HENRY CLEPPER has been executive secretary of the Society of American Foresters and managing editor of the *Journal of Forestry* since 1937. After his graduation from the Pennsylvania State Forest Academy at Mont Alto, he served for fifteen years as a forester in the Pennsylvania Department of Forests and Waters. Mr. Clepper is a contributor to *America's Natural Resources,* a contributing and consulting editor for the *Forestry Handbook,* and editor of *Careers in Conservation,* published by The Ronald Press Company.

Other Books Sponsored by the
Natural Resources Council of America

Careers in Conservation
HENRY CLEPPER, *Editor*

America's Natural Resources
CHARLES H. CALLISON, *Editor*

ORIGINS OF
AMERICAN
CONSERVATION

*Edited for the Natural Resources
Council of America*

by

HENRY CLEPPER

Society of American Foresters

THE RONALD PRESS COMPANY • NEW YORK

Library of Congress Catalog Card Number: 66–14161

PRINTED IN THE UNITED STATES OF AMERICA

To the memory of
GIFFORD PINCHOT
(1865–1946)
First American forester, and
foremost conservationist of his era

PREFACE

Many books have been written about conservation. Usually, they have to do with one resource, such as water or wildlife. They may be textbooks for instruction or more popular works for general information. Most books of this nature provide an historical account, generally brief, of the origins and development of the conservation movement in the subject under consideration.

A book that provides information about the origin of conservation in a particular field is useful to the reader to the extent that the record is authentic and reasonably complete. But, however complete the historical treatment in a book on fisheries may be, for example, it will be of little use to the seeker after information on forestry.

Some of the general books on conservation that give accounts of resource management in all fields have only limited space to chronicle historical developments. In short, they are not written as history and thus are not intended to treat of origins in the historical sense.

Although modern principles of conservation are widely understood, the evolution of the movement is not. Even among the corps of practicing conservationists, a lack of historic perspective is often evident in their writings and policies. It follows that any person concerned with conservation, whether as professional worker, interested layman, or student, will benefit by a grounding in the history of the land and its resources, and of the influences that resulted in the establishment of the several fields of resource management.

Resources workers have need for a treatise which in one handy volume will provide essential information about the origins of each of the recognized major fields of conservation. Students, teachers, and librarians also have indicated a need for such a book. Legislators have sought such source data, often unsuccessfully, as has the intelligent and curious layman whose increasing interest in all aspects of conservation, including the historical, has not been adequately satisfied by the professionals.

This book, then, is intended to fill a void. In its compilation the editors and writers had a choice: whether to produce a weighty tome with copious footnotes and all the other appurtenances of the definitive historical opus, or to tell the story of the growth of conservation in less detail than the professional historian might write it; but, nevertheless, to tell it accurately, informatively, and readably. In short, the decision was to make a worthy, though modest, contribution to American history, directed primarily to the conservation-minded reader rather than solely to the historian.

Each major field of natural resources has its own chapter. Thus the reader should have no trouble finding the salient historical origins of the subject or subjects in which his interests may lie. But if he wants to understand the historical relationships of conservation as a whole, these too are available for his perusal in other of the book's ten chapters.

Special note should be made of Chapter 10, "Next Steps for Resources." It seemed to the editors that, while a book devoted to the origins of conservation would be complete in itself, a concluding chapter would be helpful to indicate what future developments in the conservation of natural resources might be undertaken in the public interest. Thus, in a sense, this offering is not alone a look into the past and an appraisal of where we stand at present in conservation. It attempts additionally to identify important future needs as well.

Finally, a word as to what this book is not about. Its aim is to inform the reader; not to recruit him in a crusade. Its purpose is not to criticize any individual or agency, governmental or private, but rather to show that out of mistakes and indifference there arose positive action and progress.

The authors who wrote the chapters are all specialists in their respective fields. They did not compare notes because it was desired that each subject should be independently treated and should be a complete, though brief, record in itself. If there are occasional duplications and apparent similarities between one writer and another, it is but an indication that conservation, in its various manifestations, had similar origins and common goals.

This is the third book sponsored by the Natural Resources Council of America, a non-political, non-profit federation of forty national and regional associations concerned with the preservation and wise use of our renewable natural resources. Its objective is to advance the attainment of sound management of natural resources in the public interest.

For editorial advice and assistance I thank my colleagues on the Editorial Committee: Edward H. Graham of the Soil Conservation Society of America and Daniel A. Poole of the Wildlife Management Institute.

HENRY CLEPPER
Chairman of the
Editorial Committee

Washington, D.C.
January, 1966

CONTENTS

ORIGINS OF
AMERICAN CONSERVATION

CHAPTER ONE

THE CONSERVATION MOVEMENT: BIRTH AND INFANCY

Henry Clepper

Within our fifty states are the richest treasures of diversified natural resources of any nation on earth. In abundance and variety, together with favorable soil and climate, their immense wealth was the foundation of three centuries of American growth and prosperity.

John Ise, a knowledgeable writer on conservation policy, once said,

The history of the United States is fundamentally a history of rapid exploitation of immensely valuable natural resources. The possession and exploitation of these resources have given most of the distinctive traits to American character, economic development, and even political and social institutions. Whatever preeminence the United States may have among the nations of the world, in industrial activity, efficiency and enterprise, in standards of comfort in living, in wealth, and even in such social and educational institutions as are dependent upon great wealth, must be attributed to the possession of these great natural resources; and the maintenance of our preeminence in these respects is dependent upon a wise and economical use of remaining resources. Thus the question of conservation is one of the most important questions before the American people.

For more than one hundred years wasteful exploitation threatened some resources with depletion, so that intelligent action had to be taken to preserve them for future generations. Generally speaking, the public-spirited citizens who first called attention to the needless destruction of resources did not advocate, as an alternative, the hoarding of these natural assets.

ALDO LEOPOLD

1886–1948

Author of Resource Management Principles

Condemning waste and misuse, they called for wise utilization and replacement where necessary.

These public-spirited citizens did two things for which history will—or should—give suitable recognition. First, they developed the concept of conservation. Second, they worked hard for its acceptance and application.

By the closing years of the nineteenth century a group of dedicated Americans had hammered out the concept of "conservation through wise use." A persuasive and articulate spokesman for the movement was Gifford Pinchot, a forester with access to the ear of Theodore Roosevelt, whose help was solicited and enthusiastically given. Thereafter, with his dynamic leadership, the movement became a crusade. According to Aldo Leopold—another forester, teacher of game management, and convincing writer—"wildlife, forests, ranges, and waterpower were conceived by him to be *renewable organic* resources, which might last forever if they were *harvested scientifically, and not faster than they reproduced.*

" 'Conservation' had until then been a lowly word, sleeping obscurely in the dictionary. The public had never heard it. It carried no particular connotation of woods or waters. Overnight it became the label of a national issue."

How did all this come about?

Soil and water, resources and people—these are the things that constitute the history of American conservation.

What is conservation? It is a word that signifies different ideas to different people. In its most widely accepted connotation, it means the preservation and wise use of natural resources. In the terms of reference used in this book, conservation is considered as applying specifically to the renewable natural resources together with the soil and water on which they are dependent.

In contemporary usage the word was first applied to forest preservation. But it was not so used until late in the nineteenth century. Forest conservation, in the connotation of preservation and wise use, developed during the decades following the Civil War. Somewhat later in the same period, approximately the 1890's, the movement for the conservation of natural resources in general took shape.

Fortunately, for the development of the movement, the concept of conservation is easily understood. Indeed, school-children readily grasp its significance, as applied, for example, to bird life. But in its larger aspects, conservation is not simple. To understand its scope as well as its limitations, it should be considered as referring to all resources, and not to a single resource, independent of others. Thus the conservation of one resource, such as fish, is so closely related to that of another, such as water, that they are interlocking.

Our Natural Resource Heritage

Records of attempts to preserve resources are almost as old as America itself. Every schoolchild learns that the early settlers had to live off the land; that they had to get their food, clothing, shelter, and fuel from the natural resources that were so abundant all about them and without which life itself would have been impossible. Land for agriculture had to be hacked out of the wilderness by hard human labor. Thus, to the colonial farmer the forest was an obstacle to be overcome by cutting and burning. But wood was needed for homes, for charcoal, for furniture and utensils, and for boats and ship-building. In addition to wood itself, the forest yielded potash from wood ashes for making soap; pitch, rosin, tar, and turpentine; maple syrup and sugar, nuts, and fruits for food; and a host of other necessities.

Thus, it is not surprising that one of the first preservation measures was applied to trees. England, a maritime nation, wished to reserve for the Royal Navy the choicest and largest white pines in the provinces of New England. In 1691 a charter, forming certain colonies into the Province of Massachusetts, contained a provision reserving certain "royal trees" for the Crown, and officers were appointed to mark each tree so reserved with the royal symbol, a broad arrow.

Actually, similar ordinances by the colonial governments and the King were primarily police measures for the protection of property or to keep other nations from getting it. Properly speaking, they were not attempts to practice conservation, as we understand it today. For example, throughout the colonies various penalties were imposed for unauthorized timber cutting. Strict laws were enacted against woods fires. But it is doubtful that these instances were indications of regard for future timber supply. One authentic attempt at conservation was William Penn's stipulation that for every five acres cleared of forest, one acre should be left in timber. This ordinance was not long enforced.

Perhaps no single resource contributed more directly to the successful colonization of New England than its saltwater and freshwater fisheries. Applying for a royal charter to King James of England, the Pilgrims sought "leave to worship God according to their own conscience and to catch fish."

Like the aquatic and forest resources, wildlife also was essential to the settling of America. Meat for food was all important, but furs for clothing, at first used only locally, early became articles of commerce. Indeed, so important did the fur trade become that the trappers and traders were the true pioneers. The settlers, the farmers, followed them into the wilderness.

Since earliest times, travelers along the coasts and into the interior of America had marveled at the abundant fishery, wildlife, grassland, and forest resources. Their accounts are often based on wonderment rather than on scientific description. The vastness of America's natural resources was first, and most authentically, revealed by the reports of the Lewis and Clark expedition to the Pacific Northwest in 1805. So abundant as to be considered inexhaustible, these resources were free to all who could take them. Often the chronological pattern was, first, utilization; next, exploitation; and, finally, in the case of some species, extermination. Among the unpleasant and unfortunate annals of American history are the chronicles of resource destruction—the killing off of the buffalo, the disappearance of the passenger pigeon, the depletion of fisheries, the devastation of forests by logging and fire. It is not a gratifying record. It is not one of which America can be proud.

Thankfully, we shall pass over it, for our purpose is to emphasize the development of conservation, not the record of resource wastage.

This opening chapter, then, recounts the genesis of the movement, and explains how the forces came about that shaped it during the nineteenth century. Subsequent developments are described in more detail in the chapters that follow, each of which chronicles the growth of a major field of conservation.

To back up for a moment, however, at this point we should mention a remarkable book and the remarkable man who wrote it. George P. Marsh was a scholar who had keenly observed the interrelations of soil, vegetative cover, and water. In a treatise entitled *Man and Nature*, published in 1864 (in later editions it is named *The Earth as Modified by Human Action*), he explained the kind of changes, and their extent, produced by man in the physical condition of the world. He then suggested why and how resources that had been disturbed and destroyed might be restored. In short, he established the fundamental principles of conservation that exist even today.

The Dawn of Conservation

Much of the destruction of our natural resources occurred during the nineteenth century, and indeed continued into the twentieth. Forest devastation, fishery decline, wildlife extirpation, and wasteful exploitation of the range generally were rampant. The federal government did little to try to stop the trend, which, tragically, was helped along by lack of a national policy.

As was previously mentioned, the earliest attempts in American conservation were directed toward forest conservation, and these efforts were directed toward the preservation of individual species. For example, in 1828 President John Quincy Adams established a naval station and forest reservation near Pensacola, Florida, to insure a supply of live oak for the Navy. This project was short-lived, killed by official indifference.

As widespread depletion of the forest resources in various parts of the nation became evident during the mid and late 1800's, thinking people became alarmed at the wastage brought on by cutting and fire. Indeed, forest fires during that era were major calamities causing loss of human life, the wiping out of communities, and untold financial loss. A fire at Peshtigo, Wisconsin, in 1871, was a shocking example. Some 1,500 people lost their lives, and more than one million acres of timber were burned.

As will be described in more detail in Chapter 3, "Forests and Forestry," an event occurred that may be said truly to mark the beginning of the conservation era. In 1873 the American Association for the Advancement of Science memorialized the Congress and the states to pass laws for forest protection. From this action developed, two years later, the first concerted effort by a group of people to conserve a natural resource. In 1875 Dr. John A. Warder called a citizens' meeting in Chicago. It resulted in the subsequent organization of The American Forestry Association for the public advancement of forest conservation.

Out of the association emerged a ground swell of public opinion that government action should be taken to save the nation's forests, particularly the publicly owned timberlands. Bernhard E. Fernow, a trained forester from Prussia, the only forester then in the United States, joined the movement as secretary for the association. In 1886 he was designated to head the newly created Division of Forestry, which subsequently became the Forest Service, in the U.S. Department of Agriculture.

Not all government officials were indifferent to the need for conservation action. As early as 1877 Carl Schurz, Secretary of the Interior, had advocated federal forest reservations and the scientific management of timber. But the government was not the motivating force in conservation. In truth, the government did little until public-spirited citizens began to criticize it and to challenge its failure to protect forest and other resources from despoliation. There was enormous inertia to overcome. People, public officials, even scientists were indifferent. The myth prevailed that resources were inexhaustible. Catch phrases abounded—"the endless forests," "the limitless prairies," "the uncounted buffalo," "the billions of passenger pigeons," "the rivers teeming with salmon," "the ever-abundant shad."

Influence of Citizens' Associations

In 1831 a young French nobleman named Alexis de Tocqueville visited the United States. Subsequently, he wrote a book describing our developing nation, its government, customs, and people. Entitled *Democracy in America,* it commented on one aspect of our way of life that was to have a profound influence on the later development of the conservation movement. In a chapter called "Of the Use Which the Americans Make of Public Associations in Civil Life," he explains how free peoples, by associating themselves together in a common cause, can correct evils and solve the difficulties of society. "An association," he observed, "consists simply in the public assent which a number of individuals give to certain doctrines; and in the engagement which they contract to promote in a certain manner the spread of those doctrines." He went on:

Americans of all ages, all conditions, and all dispositions, constantly form associations. They have not only commercial and manufacturing companies, in which all take part, but associations of a thousand other kinds—religious, moral, serious, futile, general or restricted, enormous or diminutive. The Americans make associations to give entertainments, to found seminaries, to build inns, to construct churches, to diffuse books, to send missionaries to the antipodes; they found in this manner hospitals, prisons, and schools. If it be proposed to inculcate some truth, or to foster some feeling by the encouragement of a great example, they form a society. Wherever, at the head of some new undertaking, you see the government in France, or a man of rank in England, in the United States, you will be sure to find an association.

And so it was in conservation.

Thus the rise of the conservation movement following the Civil War was an American phenomenon in that it was started by the crusading zeal of a small group of public-spirited citizens who formed an association. Paradoxically, they demanded government protection of the nation's woodlands at a period when most people, if they thought of the matter at all, believed the nation's forests to be, for all foreseeable needs, practically inexhaustible.

Within a few years thinking people here and there throughout the country were worrying publicly about the nation's indifferent handling of other natural resources besides forests. As a case in point, during the early 1800's it had become evident that certain fisheries were declining. The valuable Atlantic salmon, for example, was disappearing from New England rivers largely as a result of dams that obstructed their spawning runs, and as a result also of siltation and pollution. Trout and other freshwater species were declining too. State legislatures were asked to enact laws to restrict the catches, to outlaw certain kinds of traps and nets, and to establish closed seasons and limits on size.

The Scientist and the Scientific Society

One of the first scientific societies organized in America for the conservation of a natural resource was the American Fisheries Society founded in 1870. Two years later Congress established the United States Fish Commission to investigate fishery problems, such as the depletion of food fishes and improvement in fish culture. In 1888 Congress authorized the President to appoint as Commissioner of Fish and Fisheries "a person of scientific and practical acquaintance with the fish and fisheries." Historically, the significance of these developments is that this federal unit began as an investigative agency staffed, at least in part, by research scientists. In due course the states followed the example of the federal government and began to set up agencies, boards, and commissions to administer their fishery resources.

In a book entitled *Conservation of Our Natural Resources*, now out of print, the editor, Loomis Havemeyer of Yale University, credited the rise of conservation to scientists. "The

modern conservation movement," he wrote, "is the direct result of the work of scientific men. The great question of conservation has been forwarded more by the rapid reduction of
our forests than by any other cause. The forests are the one
natural resource whose rapid destruction made scientists realize as early as in the seventies that, if existing practices were
continued, the end was in the not far distant future."

Another early association, organized for the advancement
of ornithological science and to foster the protection of bird
life, was the American Ornithologists Union, formed in 1883.
Among its pioneer successful efforts was the preparation of
model state laws for the protection of non-game bird species.
Within a few years New York and Pennsylvania had enacted
such legislation and by the turn of the century additional
states had followed their example.

Among these ornithologists were such scientists as A. K.
Fisher and C. Hart Merriam who while advocating laws for
bird protection were much concerned with the conservation
of wildlife in general. Out of their small beginnings evolved
what is now the U.S. Fish and Wildlife Service. It began in
1885 as the Division of Economic Ornithology and Mam-
mology, under the direction of Dr. Merriam, in the U.S. Department of Agriculture. Later the Division became the
Bureau of Biological Survey, then was renamed the Fish and
Wildlife Service and transferred to the Department of the
Interior.

Sportsmen's associations that came into existence during
the late decades of the nineteenth century were, at first, primarily concerned with the improvement of local hunting and
fishing. They worked for the passage of better state game laws
and for the more efficient enforcement of statutes already enacted. They originated much early game legislation. Thus
many state game commissions resulted from the activities of
sportsmen's associations to upgrade game protection by law
enforcement.

As time went on, these associations broadened their interests and influence by undertaking projects to educate the pub-

lic in sportsmanship and in observance of the law. In the early days, in several states, some sportsmen's organizations actually functioned as law-enforcement agencies. For example, in Delaware for forty years the Game Protective Association in effect acted in the capacity of a state game commission. In North and South Carolina the Audubon Societies assumed the duties of a game commission.

Not all these organizations devoted their interests to local or state conservation matters. Some operated on broader fronts. The Boone and Crockett Club, for instance, founded in 1885, directed its interests to the development of a national park system and to the protection of big game. Similarly, the American Game Protective Association got behind the protection of migratory birds through federal law and treaty.

In our review of these forces that constituted the conservation movement, we see always and everywhere the influence of an association or a society. The rank and file of these organizations were ordinary citizens, public-spirited to be sure, but nevertheless not otherwise distinguished. In De Tocqueville's phrase, they were "Americans of all ages, all conditions . . ." The leaders of these groups, however, numbered some of America's most dedicated men and women.

But it would be a mistake to assume that this movement resulted from the popular uprising on the part of a whole people. Actually, the contrary was true. There were comparatively few men and women working to conserve the nation's resources, and they were often exceedingly unpopular. Among some congressmen, governmental officials, and state legislatures, they were widely regarded as a nuisance.

The conservation movement of the 1800's resulted from the observations, followed by speeches and writings, of scientific men. But, important as their efforts were, they were materially forwarded by the support of hundreds—later thousands—of men and women who were not scientists and not even politically influential, but who gave liberally of their time and talents to reinforce the principle of preservation and wise use.

Modern and skeptical scholarship has shown that the flowering of the conservation movement during the latter half of the nineteenth century was a phenomenon of remarkable significance. Yet, interestingly enough, it occurred during a period almost too brief to be called historic. This movement, together with the people who worked to advance it, is one of the proudest chapters in our history. In its inception, its implementation, and its accomplishments, it has made America a fairer, richer, and happier land.

To recapitulate, as regards resource conservation, the record of the twentieth century contrasts happily with that of the nineteenth. When we look at the debit side of the record, we see the careless, wasteful, blundering exploitation of our resources as the penalty paid by a new nation to settle a raw continent. On the credit side is the gradual development of an American conservation policy, not yet perfectly realized to be sure, but continually promoted by the strenuous and idealistic action of an aroused public conscience.

For Further Reading

ALLEN, SHIRLEY W. *Conserving Natural Resources.* McGraw-Hill Book Co., Inc., New York. 1955.

CALLISON, CHARLES H. *America's Natural Resources.* The Ronald Press Co., New York. 1963.

CLEPPER, HENRY. *Careers in Conservation.* The Ronald Press Co., New York. 1963.

COYLE, DAVID CUSHMAN. *Conservation: An American Story of Conflict and Accomplishment.* Rutgers University Press, New Brunswick, N.J. 1957.

GUSTAFSON, A. F. *Conservation in the United States.* Cornell University Press, Ithaca, N.Y. 1949.

HIGHSMITH, RICHARD M. *Conservation in the United States.* Rand McNally & Co., Chicago. 1962.

LANDSBERG, HANS H., FISHMAN, L. L. and FISHER, J. L. *Resources in America's Future.* Johns Hopkins Press, Baltimore. 1963.

LIVELY, C. E., and PREISS, J. J. *Conservation Education in American Colleges.* The Ronald Press Co., New York. 1957.

RICHARDSON, ELMO R. *The Politics of Conservation: Crusades and Controversies, 1897–1913.* University of California Press, Berkeley. 1962.

SMITH, GUY H. *Conservation of Natural Resources.* John Wiley & Sons, Inc., New York. 1965.

SWAIN, DONALD C. *Federal Conservation Policy: 1921–1933.* University of California Press, Berkeley. 1963.

UDALL, STEWART L. *The Quiet Crisis.* Holt, Rinehart & Winston, Inc., New York. 1963.

CHAPTER TWO

WILDLIFE REGULATION
AND RESTORATION

James B. Trefethen

The records of America's original wildlife were written in superlatives. Even when we discount the press agentry that tinted the writings of Captain John Smith, John Josselyn, William Wood, and other seventeenth-century observers, a genuine awe of contemporary wildlife spectacles shines through their propaganda.

Josselyn's report of "hundreds" of New England wild turkeys in single flocks, Captain Arthur Barlowe's account from Jamestown of "deer, conies, hares, and fowl . . . in incredible numbers," and Wood's estimate of passenger pigeons in "millions of millions" carry a solid ring of truth. And these men saw only the fringe of a continent that contained the Great Plains—then and for two centuries longer, one of the great reservoirs of wildlife in the world.

These reports are too well documented to refute and have been repeated too often to need elaboration. Early America did produce wildlife in an abundance and variety that defied description. What is little appreciated is that wildlife is still relatively abundant today, although its composition is different from that seen by the first explorers. To understand what happened to the original wildlife, we must first know something of the changes in the American land.

When the white man arrived, he found a continent covered by climax forest and prairie grass disturbed here and there by

C. HART MERRIAM

1855–1942

Advocate of Scientific Wildlife Management

the activities of a million-odd Indians, by lightning-set fires, and by windstorms. The virgin hardwood forests of the East and Middle West supported vast flocks of passenger pigeons and the prairies' hordes of buffalo and antelope. Myriads of unspoiled marshes, ponds, sloughs, and swamps produced dense flocks of waterfowl. Millions of miles of clear streams produced beaver and otter in abundance.

Other forms of wildlife were also plentiful, but less so than the early chroniclers, through no fault of their own, would have us believe. Deer, turkeys, ruffed grouse, rabbits, and quail were abundant along the coast. They were common in natural meadows and around marshes, in old Indian clearings, and in openings created by beavers, fire, or wind. They could not have occurred in large numbers in the mature forests that blanketed most of the uplands of eastern America. Exploration, however, began on the coast and moved up the streams. Settlers were attracted naturally to any lands that were already cleared or partially cleared. They found wildlife everywhere because they traveled and settled where it was most concentrated. This rather restricted distribution also helps to account for the early decline of deer, turkeys, and other game on the eastern seaboard soon after settlement began.

Until the Revolution almost all the white population was concentrated on the seaboards of the Atlantic and the Gulf and on the Piedmont Plateau. The typical colonial farmer operated a self-sufficient family unit. He raised nearly all of his own grain, vegetables, fruit, milk, beef, wool, pork, and poultry, and he hoped for a surplus for sale or barter. He kept from one to a dozen draft horses or oxen and two or three saddle mounts. During the summer he grazed most of his livestock on common lands set aside by the town. But he had to devote much of his own acreage to oats, corn, and hay to carry his stock through the winter.

This sort of farming required large expanses of cleared and cultivated lands. As immigration swelled the population, much of the land east of the Appalachians was devoted to agriculture and grazing. Lands logged for timber or fuel were rarely permitted to revert to forest. The better lands were absorbed into farms and the poorer ones burned to encourage the growth of grass. By 1800 the only islands of virgin timber east of the mountains were in swamps or in the more remote parts of the highest hills.

In the South cultivation was even more intensive under the slave-based cotton and tobacco culture of the region. And, both North and South, what little woodland wildlife habitat that remained undisturbed by ax, fire, or livestock was hunted practically the year round.

As settlement and agriculture moved up the Mississippi and flowed across the eastern mountains, much the same process occurred in the Middle West. Under primitive conditions the best and most productive deer, turkey, and grouse range had existed along the fringes of the prairies from the southern counties of the Lake States and western Ohio southward through Illinois, Indiana, Kentucky, Tennessee, and eastern Missouri. The virgin oak-hickory-beech forests east and north of this intermediate zone between forest and prairie produced the great flights of passenger pigeons. These zones also contained some of the most fertile croplands in America. The prairie woodlands were cleared and the soil broken by the plow or grazed by livestock. The cutting of the hardwood forests contributed as much to the extermination of the passenger pigeon as the market hunting that harassed it almost to the end.

Forty years after the close of the Revolution much of America east of the Mississippi was under cultivation. By 1825, for example, all but a small part of the Great Smoky Mountains had been cleared for grazing or farming.

With the opening of the Great Plains a final phase in the reshaping of the American landscape began. Homesteaders, miners, ranchers poured out over the prairies to stake their claims and make their fortunes. Twenty years after the Civil War most of the face of the continent had been altered completely. Only fragments of the original forests and prairie remained unmodified by man. Hence, the wildlife changed too.

Era of Wildlife Decline

The more conspicuous forms of America's original wilderness wildlife hit their low point between 1880 and 1890. The passenger pigeon and the buffalo hovered on the brink of extermination. The white-tailed deer and the wild turkey had been eliminated nearly everywhere east of the Rockies. The elk, which had once ranged east to the Appalachians, has been pushed back to a few strongholds in the western mountains. Antelope were still declining and numbered about 50,000. In all of New England deer remained common only in northern Maine and on part of Cape Cod. Between Lake Erie and Lake Ontario and Virginia the only large tract of occupied deer range was in the northern Adirondacks. In the South whitetails occupied scattered coastal swamps from Virginia to Florida and along the Gulf to Texas. A fair population survived in the northern Lake States and in the jungle-like bottomlands of the lower Mississippi River. By 1890, there were only about 500,000 deer in North America.

Habitat change, of course, was not the only reason for this decline. Throughout nearly three centuries, America's wildlife had been subjected to merciless persecution. The pioneer's outlook toward wildlife was totally pragmatic. The beasts of the forests and the fowls of the air were part of the bounty of God placed on earth for the use of man. And use them he did!

The first settlers were tradesmen and farmers rather than hunters. But in the New World they found a people who were among the most skillful hunters on earth. Before the arrival of the whites, the Indian had hunted only for his own limited needs. Some tribes even had rudimentary game laws based on taboos. But as soon as he learned the profit motive, the native hunter became a deadly Nemesis of any wildlife he could trade for ax, gun, or string of beads. He knew how to run down deer on crusted snow, to snare deer and turkeys, to spear beaver in their lodges, and to suffocate passenger pigeon squabs with smudge fires.

By the end of the seventeenth century the Indian had been pushed westward, but his place was taken by white hunters who had learned from him and refined his techniques. The market hunters were in the vanguard of civilization's march toward the West. And they were systematic killers who hunted at all seasons without regard for the future. The settlers who followed them, living off the land until they became established, usually eliminated most of the local big game that was left and then modified the habitat with ax, plow, and cow.

If the original wildlife had been universally abundant, the relatively few hunters before 1880 could have made only small inroads on its numbers. But the gregarious buffalo traveled in great herds that mounted hunters could harass at will. The passenger pigeon concentrated in breeding roosts of unbelievable density, with up to 100 nests in a single tree. Beaver were found principally along narrow streams. Deer frequented the relatively limited undisturbed brushlands. All these species, in the absence of effective game laws, could be systematically eliminated from a given locality by a relatively few hunters in a short period of time.

The worst aspect of hunting as it existed in America before the Civil War was that it was usually carried on well into the breeding and nesting seasons of the game. The constant harassment of nesting birds and mammals with young was a major factor in the decline of a number of species. It was a principal cause of the extermination of the passenger pigeon.

But hunting could not have been the only reason for the decline. While many species were becoming scarce, a reverse trend was taking place in others. Bobwhite quail, fox squirrels, cottontail rabbits, red foxes, and similar farm wildlife, according to historical evidence, reached their highest point of abundance while the deer were nearing their lowest ebb. The varied agriculture of the East and Middle West produced a patchwork of pasture, cropland, woodlot, orchard, and hayfield separated by hedges, brushy fencerows, and overgrown walls. It was ideal habitat for farm wildlife, and the species in this category increased although they were persecuted by market hunters and meat hunters along with the others.

Early Protective Laws

Laws to protect deer appear in many colonial legal codes. The first, providing for a six-month closure in deer hunting, was written into the town charter of Newport, Rhode Island, in 1639, and extended colony-wide in 1646. Connecticut and Massachusetts adopted similar laws in 1698. By 1750 most of the original colonies had similar laws. Unfortunately, the date of each of these laws reflects the date when deer became scarce rather than a turning point for the better in the status of the species. A Massachusetts law of 1715 authorized the towns to appoint local officers known as "deer reeves" to prosecute offenders. This office, too, was adopted by other colonies. But in many towns, deer reeves were appointed after there were no deer to protect. The backwoods towns, which had deer, either ignored the law or appointed men who could be trusted not to enforce it.

These laws are interesting legal curiosities. But they had little application under the hard-scrabble conditions of the frontier. Their real value was that they remained in the legal codes of the colonies and became part of the common law of the original states. As such they served as precedents for more realistic game regulations after wildlife restoration began.

Deer were about the only animals that the colonists made any effort to protect. Most of the other laws affecting wildlife encouraged the killing of wolves and other predators and farm pests. One interesting exception was an ordinance in 1733 in New York protecting "the breed of English Pheasants in the Colony."

The first-known state game law adopted after the Revolution provided for a closed season on ruffed grouse on Long Island, New York. Maine, in 1826, enacted a closed season of

6½ months on deer and moose. Maryland was the first state, in 1842, to try to regulate waterfowl hunting. These laws, like their colonial predecessors, failed because of inadequate public support.

The Stir of Conservation

It was not until around 1850 that the first articulate voices in support of wildlife conservation were raised. Henry David Thoreau and his intellectual associates in Concord and Boston attacked the problem on the aesthetic front, giving Americans an appreciation for nature that they lacked before. Henry William Herbert ("Frank Forester"), the first vocal spokesman for the American sportsman, hammered at the theme that game animals had more value for sport than they did for meat. Among his disciples was an influential group of sportsmen in New York City who had banded together in 1844 to form the New York Sporting Club. A few years later they reorganized it to form the New York State Game Protective Association, the first private conservation organization in America. After 1850 sportsmen in other states formed similar associations. While their primary function was to obtain restrictions against the market hunter, many assumed quasi-police powers in enforcing existing laws.

State fish-and-wildlife administration originated in Massachusetts in 1865 when the legislature authorized the creation of a fish commission. Its powers were soon broadened to include authority over game birds and mammals. Within a few years most of the states had comparable agencies. The early fish-and-game commissioners had little power and low budgets, but they were instrumental in expanding the legal protection for wildlife.

These efforts after 1870, received eloquent encouragement from the first American sporting journals, particularly *Forest and Stream*, published and edited by Charles Hallock, and *Shooting and Fishing*, under Arthur Corbin Gould. Hallock, Gould, and George Bird Grinnell, Hallock's successor, were scientists and sportsmen as well as editors and writers. All were members of the American Ornithologists Union, which in 1885 adopted a model state game-bird law and recommended the appropriation by Congress of funds for studies in "entomology, economic ornithology, and mammalogy." This was the origin of the United States Biological Survey, which was organized in the Department of Agriculture four years later. Although it was a research agency without police powers, it did much to coordinate and broaden the growing interest in wildlife in America.

In 1886 Grinnell founded the New York Audubon Society, the first such group in the United States and one which soon had counterparts in other states. In 1888 Grinnell became a charter member of Theodore Roosevelt's Boone and Crockett Club. Although limited to 100 active members, all of whom were big-game hunters, and about half as many associates, the Boone and Crockett Club was influential out of proportion to its size. Its select membership contained some of the most prominent political, scientific, and literary figures of the day. Under Roosevelt's dynamic leadership it became one of the most influential forces for conservation.

Evils of Market Hunting

The rather strangely assorted leaders of the early conservation movement were unanimous on one point—that the market hunter had to go. Market gunners were increasing in numbers with the population growth, and, with the virtual extermination of the buffalo and passenger pigeon, were turning to other game. Improvements in transportation permitted them to invade the last strongholds of the mule deer, elk, and mountain sheep in the West. Trainloads of ducks, geese, cranes, plovers, and prairie chickens were arriving each week from the Great Plains at processing centers in Kansas City and Chicago, and less adventuresome hunters were beating the coverts nearer home for quail, ruffed grouse, woodcock, and snipe. Under this onslaught species that had increased in abundance over the years also began to decline. Market hunters were invading the breeding grounds of the migratory waterfowl in the North, disrupting nesting activity and killing paired birds. Everywhere spring hunting for ducks, geese, and shorebirds had been traditional for centuries.

Shortly before 1890, fashion decreed that women's hats should be adorned with fine feathers. Market hunters, sensing a new source of profit, immediately invaded the great nesting rookeries of the southern swamps. They slaughtered hundreds of thousands of nesting egrets, herons, ibises, and other wading birds for their plumage. Millions of nestlings, deprived of parents, died. And no bird, regardless of size, was safe if it sported bright feathers.

This was the straw that broke the back of the market hunter's camel. Public sentiment had been hardening slowly against him. And now people who thought nothing of buying grouse or canvasbacks in the local market were sickened by the slaughter of orioles, warblers, and swallows.

On May 25, 1900, Congress passed the Lacey Act. Written by Congressman John F. Lacey of Iowa, it was the first federal law dealing with wildlife on the national level. It made the interstate shipment of game killed in violation of state law a federal offense. Its immediate effect was to choke off much of the traffic in wild meat and plumage that the market gunners had carried on in defiance of state law.

Refuges for Wildlife

In the meantime another concept of wildlife protection had taken form. This was the refuge movement, which originated in 1872 when Congress set aside Yellowstone National Park as a "pleasuring ground for the people." Although the park was created because of its unique hot springs and geysers, it served as a haven during the next few decades for the only significant herd of wild buffalo left in the United States. Poachers continued to harass the buffalo in the park after those on the plains had been eliminated. In the absence of specific law, even the

Army, which detailed soldiers to protect the park, was unable to check the killing of its wildlife.

The Boone and Crockett Club allied itself with various scientific organizations to obtain protection for the wildlife in Yellowstone Park. On May 7, 1894, the Yellowstone Park Protective Bill, also written by Lacey, became law. Among other things it provided jail sentences of up to two years for anyone convicted of killing wildlife in Yellowstone Park.

The demonstrated value of Yellowstone as a wildlife refuge led Roosevelt and his associates to suggest making all the new national-forest reservations inviolate wildlife refuges under military protection. The impracticality of this approach was recognized by Gifford Pinchot, who convinced Roosevelt that the same ends could be achieved by making only parts of the national forests wildlife refuges. By preserving large blocks of forest habitat, however, the forest reservations helped carry breeding stocks of America's largest wildlife through the critical 1890's. When Roosevelt became President, he used his powers to establish national wildlife refuges. In 1903 he created Pelican Island National Wildlife Refuge in Florida as a sanctuary for sea birds threatened by plume hunters. Some of the national forest areas that Roosevelt set aside were selected as much for their value to wildlife as they were for timber.

Laws with Teeth

By 1905 the modern wildlife-conservation movement had begun to take form. Most of its elements—laws and enforcements, refuges, protection for breeding stocks, state and federal administration—were recognizable, but the whole was uncoordinated and loosely organized. The Conference of Governors, called by Roosevelt in 1908, was the catalyst that pulled the various parts into perspective and molded them into a unified structure. Although the White House Conference dealt with wildlife only in passing, it stimulated the growth of state wildlife agencies throughout the nation. State officials, who in the past had gone their separate ways, began to compare notes and to borrow progressive ideas from their neighbors. This strengthened a liaison that had begun in 1902 with the establishment of the International Association of Game, Fish and Conservation Commissioners.

One of the glaring weaknesses of the wildlife-conservation movement at that time was a general lack of protection for migratory game birds. Only Canada and the northern states produced ducks, geese, and shorebirds in sizable numbers. In the fall the birds moved southward, passing successively from one state line across to the next in their migration. No one state could claim them; none would assume responsibility for their protection. Few were willing to impose restrictions on their own hunters while those in neighboring states were permitted wide-open seasons and bag limits. The only solution was federal regulation.

The first bill to achieve this end was introduced in Congress on December 5, 1904, by Congressman George Shiras III of Pennsylvania. This and later attempts failed because of doubts concerning their constitutionality.

In 1911 the American Game Protective and Propagation Association came into being. It was a sportsmen-supported organization with a professional staff headed by John B. Burnham, the former chief game protector of New York. One of its first missions was to secure the enactment of a federal migratory-game-bird law. In 1912 three bills, all patterned after the Shiras Bill, were introduced in Congress. But this time the bills had overwhelming public support. The National Audubon Society, which had been established in 1902, marshaled the bird lovers while the American Game Association organized support among the sportsmen and state wildlife administrators. Henry Ford assigned one of his top advertising executives to Washington to get the bill through Congress. The Weeks-McLean Law was signed on March 4, 1913, by President Taft on the day he left office.

But the law was of questionable constitutionality. Some states ignored it completely, confident that it would never pass the test of court scrutiny. In the meantime, however, on January 14, 1913, at the height of the debate over the bill in Congress, Senator Elihu Root had introduced a Senate resolution authorizing the President of the United States to negotiate a bird treaty with Great Britain. It contained all the salient features of the Weeks-McLean Bill. A version of Root's resolution was introduced as a bill in the Senate on April 7 by Senator George P. McLean, a coauthor of the controversial law. A few days later a bill to repeal the Weeks-McLean Law went into the Congressional hopper. The Migratory Treaty between the United States and Great Britain to protect migratory birds in Canada and the United States was signed on August 16, 1916. The enabling Act that made it effective passed on July 3, 1918. The treaty gave the entire question new perspective. There is little doubt but that the Supreme Court would have declared the Weeks-McLean Law unconstitutional. But in the famous test case *Missouri vs. Holland* it found the treaty inviolate and the question of the Weeks-McLean Law to be moot.

The Migratory Bird Treaty Act was one of the most important pieces of legislature ever passed for wildlife. It immediately ended spring hunting and the sale of migratory game birds. It ended the hunting of plovers, sandpipers, and most other shorebirds, and placed all migratory insectivorous birds and songbirds as well as threatened species under federal protection. It provided for regulated hunting of ducks, geese, woodcock, snipe, doves, and other game birds at the discretion of the Secretary of Agriculture. And it reaffirmed the authority of the federal government to enforce such regulations.

Patterns of Shifting Land Use

While this long legislative battle was being fought, other changes had been taking place in the American landscape and the American economy. The self-sufficient family farm of the East had been declining ever since the Civil War. Many farmers had moved West or into the growing towns and cities. Those who remained on the land began to specialize. Sheep and beef cattle all but disappeared from eastern farms. Farmers found it cheaper to buy western grain than to raise their own. Thus hundreds of thousands of acres that had been tilled or grazed for centuries were released from use. When automotive power began to replace horses, still more acreage was retired. As the land was idled, forests gradually replaced fields and pastures.

On much of this abandoned land, particularly along the coastal plain and throughout much of New England, the new forests consisted primarily of "old field" pine—white pine in the North; slash, loblolly, Virginia, and shortleaf pines farther south. They provided little food for wildlife. But as soon as they matured, extensive logging operations started. A few years later the cutover lands supported another type of young growth, predominantly oak, birch, maple, hickory, and other hardwoods mixed with scattered conifers—ideal habitat for deer, grouse, and other forest wildlife.

By 1900 most of the eastern states had relegated big-game hunting to past history. The majority had no deer at all, although they did have laws to protect them. From the pockets of range where they had weathered the low level of the 1890's, deer began to spread to occupy the new habitat created by land abandonment. To accelerate the spread, sportsmen's organizations and state game agencies began to purchase deer from the owners of deer parks or from states, like Michigan, where deer had remained relatively abundant. By this time the state game agencies had developed legal muscle and were able to provide adequate protection for the expanding deer herds.

The return of the deer was one of the most spectacular developments in wildlife history. The case of Pennsylvania is typical. In 1900 a live deer in the Keystone State was a curiosity. In 1907, when the state opened its first modern deer season, hunters killed 200. By 1923, the reported legal kill had climbed to 3,239. In 1963 hunters took 84,416 from a herd estimated at 425,000! And with the deer, ruffed grouse, black bears, wild turkeys, and other wildlife began to return to places where they had been absent for a century or more.

Importation and Propagation

On the credit side of the ledger, too, at this time was the phenomenal spread of the Chinese ring-necked pheasant across the northern states and southern Canada. English pheasants had been tried unsuccessfully in New York, New Hampshire, and New Jersey as early as the eighteenth century. Then in 1881, Judge O. N. Denny brought back from Shanghai between 16 and 25 pairs of Chinese ringnecks and released them in Oregon's Willamette Valley. The corn-wheat agriculture, which was replacing the virgin prairie and destroying the habitat of the native prairie chicken, provided an ideal home for the pheasant. Aided by a few additional importations, transplants, and the release of pen-raised birds, the ringneck spread rapidly across the continent, reaching the East Coast before 1900. By that time the foreigner was providing annual hunting throughout much of the Corn Belt.

This opened new vistas for the state fish and game agencies. Nearly all began to raise pheasants and to experiment with other foreign game. Japanese quail, chukar partridges from India, and Hungarian partridges were released in large numbers in almost all states but succeeded in establishing themselves only locally. The imported quail disappeared entirely. Bobwhite and wild turkeys were raised and released by hundreds of thousands in an effort to increase native game stocks. Much money was wasted in trying to raise ruffed grouse, prairie chickens, and cottontail rabbits, none of which lends itself to artificial rearing. The deliberations of the National Conference on Game Breeding, held in 1915, centered around this aspect of wildlife management. It was the forerunner of the modern North American Wildlife and Natural Resources Conference.

Problems of Too Much Protection

A second point of emphasis in the development of wildlife management was predator control. The practice was as old as American history. The first settlers had paid cash awards to people who killed wolves and other predators that threatened livestock. Later the bounty was revived in an effort to protect wildlife. Kill foxes, and there will be more quail; kill bobcats and coyotes, and there will be more deer. In the absence of scientific studies, the more subtle interrelationships of predator, prey, and habitat were generally overlooked.

The early game administrators had other pat solutions that still plague their modern counterparts. The return of the deer coincided with restrictions on hunting. By this time the majority of the states where hunting seasons had not reopened permitted the killing of only antlered bucks. Since deer were increasing rapidly, it was assumed that the buck law, alone, was responsible. The basic cause, the return of suitable cover, was largely overlooked. From underprotection many of the states began to err on the side of overprotection.

The first trouble appeared on Arizona's Kaibab Plateau where Theodore Roosevelt had created one of the first big-game refuges in the United States, and in Yellowstone National Park. In both places wildlife enjoyed absolute protection from hunting. Extensive trapping by government hunters had removed nearly all the larger predators. By 1911 the elk in Yellowstone had increased to the point where they were endangering their natural food supplies, and park rangers were resorting to winter feeding. Between 1906 and 1920 the Kaibab mule-deer herd increased from 3,000 to 30,000, although unofficial estimates placed their numbers as high as 100,000. In 1924 deer began to die by the thousands in Pennsylvania, where twenty years earlier, there had been no deer. By that time, in spite of annual hunting for bucks, the population had zoomed close to the million mark.

These were problems that none of the early game officials could have foreseen. For the first time it became apparent that there could be such a thing as too many deer. But it was easier to convince the public on the need for protection than for deer-population control. Some state administrators did not even try. The phenomenon was beyond their comprehension and contrary to all they had been led to believe.

Birth of Wildlife Management

The first man to explain matters clearly was Aldo Leopold, a forester whose vocation was the study of wildlife. In 1925 he expounded a theory on game management based on the interrelationships of wildlife-population dynamics and habitat. His theory, published in the *Bulletin* of the American Game Association, became the foundation of modern scientific wildlife management. In 1929 Leopold was engaged by the University of Wisconsin for lectures on game management. The course was so productive that he was appointed a professor of game management in the first such chair in North America. His lectures formed the basis for *Game Management*, published in 1933, still one of the basic texts in the field.

In essence, Leopold taught that the quality and quantity of habitat govern the number of wild animals that a given area can support; that each wild population produces a generous surplus over that needed to maintain adequate stocks; and that this surplus can be removed by hunters without endangering the species. If it is not used by hunters, it will die of other causes, some of which may endanger the breeding stocks more seriously than regulated hunting. In both Pennsylvania and the Kaibab Plateau exactly that happened with the deer. The liberalized deer seasons of the present reflect a recognition of Leopold's philosophies.

Saving the Waterfowl

Throughout much of the 1920's the concern of wildlife conservationists centered on waterfowl. Since the turn of the century agricultural drainage had been making inroads into the wetlands of America, hunters were increasing in numbers, and duck flights had begun to drop. Conservationists for years had been trying to obtain a system of waterfowl refuges where ducks could breed and winter without disturbance. Disagreement over financing and the management of the proposed refuges had led to deep splits between the conservationists themselves. The first fruits of this concern was the enactment in June, 1924, of the Upper Mississippi Refuge Act. It authorized Congress to appropriate $1 million to purchase bottomlands as waterfowl refuges along the upper reaches of the Mississippi. But even this program was hamstrung by a lack of appropriations; moreover, it was inadequate for the job.

Then the worst drought in American history struck the prairies and dust clouds darkened the continent. Waterfowl flights dropped to trickles. In the face of this emergency conservationists unified behind a general waterfowl-conservation program. The Norbeck-Andresen Act of February 18, 1929, authorized federal funds for a national system of waterfowl refuges and established the Migratory Bird Conservation Committee comprised of members of the President's cabinet.

But because of the national economic depression Congress was slow to implement the Norbeck-Andresen Act. Income from taxes dropped with the economy and general funds could not be spared for what many regarded as frills. But Congress did pick up an idea that had been advanced ten years earlier to permit hunters to pay for the projects. In 1934 it enacted the Duck Stamp Act, which required all waterfowl hunters sixteen years of age or older to purchase a special $1 stamp. The proceeds were earmarked for waterfowl restoration. In its first year it brought $600,000; but since that time, with the price raised to $3, it has contributed up to $6 million annually.

The first chief of the Bureau of Biological Survey appointed under the administration of Franklin Delano Roosevelt was a dynamic cartoonist from Iowa, Jay N. "Ding" Darling. He had been one of the outstanding critics of the waterfowl-conservation program. Darling was a man of boundless energy, bril-

liant imagination, and unlimited courage. He reduced the
open seasons and bag limits, cracked down on bootleg market
hunters, and outlawed live decoys, baiting, and other practices
that had been traditional for years. He fought successfully
for additional funds for wildlife.

Progress Accelerates

In 1935 Darling launched the Cooperative Wildlife Research Unit Program, a system of training and research stations for advanced students in wildlife management at various
land-grant colleges across the nation. They were financed
jointly by the Bureau of Biological Survey, the respective state
fish-and-game agency and land-grant college, and the American Wildlife Institute (later the Wildlife Management Institute). The units were able to conduct important research
projects while training graduate students to enter professional
service.

Darling also was responsible for President Roosevelt's calling of the First North American Wildlife Conference, a much
broadened version of the old American Game Conference.
Held in 1936, it brought together biologists, administrators, and
sportsmen to discuss new approaches to wildlife conservation.
Thereafter it was continued on an annual basis under the
auspices of the American Wildlife Institute and its successor,
the Wildlife Management Institute. Darling also established
the National Wildlife Federation to unify and coordinate the
activities of local and state conservation groups.

One of the most far-reaching pieces of wildlife legislation
was the Pittman-Robertson Federal Aid in Wildlife Restoration Act of 1937. It allocated back to the states all revenues
collected under the 11 per cent federal excise tax on sporting
arms and ammunition. Each state received its annual appor-
tionment under a formula based on the number of licensed
hunters and the area of the state. More than $14 million have
been available to the states and territories in some recent years

for approved projects, wildlife research, land acquisition, and development. An important clause in this law requires the states to apply all of their hunting-license fees to the operation of the fish-and-wildlife agency and its programs. Before 1937 it was a common practice for state legislatures to divert hunting-license revenues to highway and school programs.

On June 30, 1940, the U.S. Fish and Wildlife Service was established in the Department of the Interior by consolidating the former Bureau of Biological Survey from the Department of Agriculture and the Bureau of Fisheries from the Department of Commerce. Ira N. Gabrielson, who had succeeded Darling as chief of the Bureau of Biological Survey, became its first director.

These were the basic developments that molded the wildlife-conservation movement as we know it today. The typical state has a strong, well-financed wildlife agency staffed by specialists in research, management, law enforcement, and administration, supported almost entirely by sportsmen's fees. Hunting seasons are established on the basis of the annual supply of game determined by careful study to minimize danger to breeding stocks. Nearly all maintain wildlife refuges in extensive habitat-restoration programs in private and public lands. The U.S. Forest Service and the Soil Conservation Service through their own staffs of wildlife specialists maintain close liaison with state wildlife officials. Practically all projects that benefit game birds and mammals also benefit song and insectivorous birds.

At the national level the Fish and Wildlife Service is responsible for protecting all birds that regularly pass in normal migration across state or international borders. It is also entrusted with the responsibility for preserving endangered species, such as the whooping crane, trumpeter swan, and Key deer. The Secretary of the Interior, in consultation with experts in and out of government service, sets annual hunting regulations on migratory game birds on the basis of supply and the anticipated demand.

Goals Have Been Won

With this pattern established, where do we stand today? Certainly the expression "vanishing wildlife" that was so popular and so appropriate a generation or two ago applies today to a relatively few species. Deer and wild turkeys have been restored to abundance in many places where the pioneers never saw a deer or a turkey. The 1963 inventory of big game, compiled by the Bureau of Sport Fisheries and Wildlife, indicates a population of deer in the United States in excess of 14 million, where in 1890 it was about 500,000. Antelope have increased more than twentyfold since 1920, and more elk are taken each year by hunters than existed in all of North America in 1900. Even the buffalo, which at one time numbered only 500, now numbers in the thousands.

Upland game is also abundant. One might point to the decline of the prairie chicken on the western plains while overlooking the spectacular numbers of ring-necked pheasants that occupy its former range. One might lament the extinct passenger pigeon and ignore the millions of mourning doves and bobwhite quail that exist where none lived in the days of the pioneers.

This is not to say that the loss of the passenger pigeon was not a major tragedy or that every effort should not be made to prevent further losses of prairie chickens, whooping cranes, California condors, and other threatened species. But these are wilderness species that could be restored to abundance only by converting large blocks of prosperous country back to a wilderness condition. Of the approximately sixty species and subspecies listed as "threatened," none was ever hunted intensively for sport. They are threatened today by habitat changes wrought by man. The best that can be done is to maintain in parks and refuges living samples of these birds and mammals for the pleasure and knowledge of the Americans of tomorrow. America cannot support 200 million people in prosperity and still have 200 million buffalo. But we can have millions of deer, wild turkey, antelope, pheasant, bob-white quail, mourning dove, and other species that can thrive in an environment molded by human beings. We can even maintain spectacular flights of ducks and geese and shorebirds, which as a group, are most heavily threatened by the activities of man.

America's wildlife biologists and administrators have the knowledge that is needed to accomplish these results and much of the necessary legal authority. All they need are the under-standing and support of the general public.

For Further Reading

ALLEN, DURWARD L. *Our Wildlife Legacy.* Funk & Wagnalls Co., New York. 1962.

DAY, ALBERT M. *North American Waterfowl.* The Stackpole Co., Harrisburg, Pa. 1959.

GABRIELSON, IRA N. *Wildlife Conservation.* The Macmillan Co., New York. 1959.

LEOPOLD, ALDO. *Game Management.* Charles Scribner's Sons, New York. 1933.

MATTHIESEN, PETER. *Wildlife in America.* The Viking Press, New York. 1959.

TREFETHEN, JAMES B. *Crusade for Wildlife.* The Stackpole Co., Harrisburg, Pa. 1961.

CHAPTER THREE

FORESTS AND FORESTRY

Arthur B. Meyer

The prodigious wealth of natural resources of the North American continent made possible the astonishing mushroom growth of a new nation. No small part of those resources was the supply of timber. Timber for homes, for warmth, for transport, for the fashioning of tools—for these the colonists, and after them the westward-moving settlers, looked to the forests.

Colonial Times

Early in the history of the colonies the British government adopted a policy of reserving for use of the Royal Navy a future supply of naval stores, tall pines for ship masts and pitch pines for tar. As early as 1626 Plymouth Colony passed an ordinance pointing out the "inconvenience likely to arise" from a lack of timber and stating that no one should sell timber out of the colony without approval of the authorities. Ten years later this ordinance was revised to forbid sale of timber cut from lands reserved for the public use without official sanction. Numerous and diverse laws by the colonies forbade, established fines, or otherwise sought to control available timber supplies and to prevent trespass on public lands.

Strict laws against forest fires were passed by several of the colonies in New England prior to 1650. A Massachusetts law of 1743 specifically recognized fire damage to young tree growth and the soil. In 1681 William Penn in his ordinance for the disposal of lands required that for every five acres cleared of forests one acre should be left in forest. The Germans who came to Pennsylvania are the only settlers his-

GIFFORD PINCHOT

1865–1946

Premier American Forester

torically credited with economy in the use of wood even though
it was abundant.

It is difficult indeed to find any but the most tenuous relationship between the precepts of forest conservation as we
know them today and the attitude and actions of the colonists
dealing with the forest. Primarily, they were concerned with
easy availability of wood for ordinary use and preservation of
particular species adapted to special uses. The population
was confined mainly to the Atlantic Coast and the extent of the
inland forests unknown; only supplies of timber adjacent to
water transport were available. Wood was a necessity in almost every aspect of everyday living.

Naval Reserves

The need to protect American merchant vessels from Al-
gerian pirates and aggressions of the French Navy led to Congressional actions in 1794 and 1798 authorizing the President
to provide warships for protection. The building of the vessels
caused government officials to consider the necessity of making
provisions for a future supply of timber for defense, thus
bringing about the first action of the United States government regarding timberlands. In 1799 Congress appropriated
$200,000 for the purchase and reservation of timber or timber-
land suitable for the Navy. Little was done at the time because live oak was considered the prime timber and most of
that then known to exist was in Florida and Louisiana, and in
foreign hands. Two tracts totaling 1,950 acres on two islands
on the Georgia coast, however, were purchased.

After the War of 1812 the United States entered on a policy
of naval expansion and an Act of 1817 authorized the Secretary
of the Navy to select tracts of land producing oak and redcedar,
and imposing a penalty on cutting such timber from these
lands or any other public lands of the United States.

When Spain ceded Florida to the United States in 1819, it
was discovered that live oak was being destroyed by tres-
passers, and the President was empowered to use military
force to stop it. In 1827 the President was authorized to take

proper measures to preserve oak timbers on the public lands and, further, to reserve such lands anywhere on the public domain. More funds were appropriated for the purchase of live-oak timberlands. Not only were provisions for land reservations made, but in Florida the government undertook experiments in transplanting and cultivating live oak. Short lived as these experiments were, they were the first governmental effort in forestry research in the United States.

In 1831 further efforts to protect reserved timber resulted in a law that superseded the oak-and-redcedar prohibition of the 1817 Act. The new law forbade the removal of oak and cedar or any other timber from these reserved lands, or from any other lands of the United States.

Under these various Acts a small amount of timberland was reserved in parcels in Georgia, Florida, Alabama, Mississippi, and Louisiana. But apparently the government was almost powerless to prevent trespass by timber thieves and the encroachment of settlers. It began disposing some of the lands in 1843 and had finished the task except for a few small tracts in Louisiana following the Civil War. The development of iron ships during and subsequent to the Civil War ended the government's concern with shipbuilding timbers as a strategic material.

This passing phase of forest history marks the first attempt by the federal government to reserve lands for their timber values, to experiment in artificial means of growing a wanted species, and of the first appropriations for the protection of timberlands.

From the Atlantic Westward

It is apparent that early concern with timber resources in the colonies and after independence was based primarily upon fear of scarcity. The introduction in the East of coal for fuel, railroads for transport, and later of iron ships, each contributed to a lessened dependence upon wood and therefore to less worry over possible short supply. But undoubtedly the one historical fact that most influenced our national attitude toward the forest during the first three-fourths of the nineteenth century resulted from the movement of settlement throughout the vast forested eastern half of what is now the United States. Between 1820 and 1870 the population of the country more than quadrupled.

Innumerable farms were carved out of the forest, and the timber burned in the lack of ready markets. Plows scratched between deadened tree trunks when more hasty measures were called for. Fires were set in the underbrush with wanton carelessness. The forests were an impediment to settlement and agriculture. They were not looked upon with concern or even favor by the man seeking to establish a home and a living in the vast timbered areas.

Simultaneously with the rapid expansion of settlement of the country, and essential to that expansion, was a mushrooming lumbering industry.

From a production figure of one billion board feet in 1840, U.S. sawmills turned out 35 billion in 1869, and reached an all-time peak of 46 billion in 1906 and again in 1907. The center of the industry moved during this period from Maine to New York (1850) to Pennsylvania (1860), and to the Lake States (1870). Subsequently it centered in the South and then moved on to the far West. Everything seemed to combine to bring about forest depletion. The government sought means for hasty disposal of the lands. The settlers rushed to get it cleared and in crops for agriculture. There was an enormous demand for new homes that rapid developments in lumbering techniques and the railroad industry successfully supplied.

That the forest resources should have been used to develop the country no one would deny. But that such use was characterized by wasteful exploitation of the forest, usually followed by fire, is the painful record.

A Start To Rectify

In most, if not all, fields of natural-resource conservation the threat of depletion, or at least reduction of plentifulness, produces the first spark. Refinements of conservation concepts follow.

In 1873 the American Association for the Advancement of Science appointed a "committee to memorialize Congress and the several state legislatures upon the importance of promoting the cultivation of timber and the preservation of forests and to recommend proper legislation for securing these objects." The American Forestry Association was organized in 1875 for the promotion of forestry and timber culture. It sponsored the first American Forest Congress in 1882 in which governors of various states participated. Various other private organizations became interested in forestry during the same period and conducted educational campaigns.

As a result of public concern, Congress provided in 1876 for the appointment of a forestry agent in the Department of Agriculture to study and report on the forest situation and the means best adapted to the preservation and renewals of forests. The man appointed was Franklin B. Hough, one of the leading proponents of government action in forestry. The three reports developed by Dr. Hough did much to increase public sentiment for forest conservation. The forestry office was made the Division of Forestry in 1881. Hough was succeeded by Nathaniel H. Egleston in 1883, and in 1886 Bernhard E. Fernow became Division Chief.

In March of 1891 Congress passed a law authorizing the President to set aside specific areas in the public domain as forest reserves. The first reserve, covering more than 1.25 million acres in Wyoming, was proclaimed that year. During the administrations of Presidents Harrison and Cleveland some 33 million acres of forest reserves were established in the western states. No provisions, however, were made for their management until 1897 when Congress authorized a system of organization and administration under the jurisdiction of the General Land Office, Department of the Interior.

The first attempt actually to practice forestry in the United States, during the 1890's, was conducted on privately owned land, the 7,000-acre forest on George W. Vanderbilt's Biltmore estate in western North Carolina. Gifford Pinchot, the first American-born, professionally educated (in Europe) forester, was employed to manage the property. In 1898 Carl A. Schenck, a German forester who had succeeded Pinchot on the estate, opened the Biltmore Forest School as a private academy for practical training in forestry. In that same year, a College of Forestry was established at Cornell University. In the fall of 1900 Yale University began a graduate program of training in professional forestry.

It is interesting to note that as early as 1885 four states created commissions to deal with forest and watershed protection—California, Colorado, Ohio, and New York. Only the New York agency continued in unbroken existence, but at least the concept of state action had been born.

And so the stage was set for the struggles and the triumphs of forest conservation in the twentieth century.

From 1900 to 1910

By 1900 the Division of Forestry in the Department of Agriculture, under the leadership of Gifford Pinchot since 1898, employed 123 persons. The staff included about 60 "student assistants," many of whom ultimately became professional foresters, and also some prominent scientists from universities and colleges on a part-time-collaborator basis. The budget that year was $48,520. The work of the Division consisted of education, research, and cooperation with private owners in applying forest-management practices.

In his first message to Congress, in 1901, President Theodore Roosevelt recommended the transfer of the forest reserves from the Department of the Interior to the Department of Agriculture, to be administered by the Bureau of Forestry, recently advanced in rank from a division. The change, however, was not accomplished until 1905 when the necessary legislation was passed. Simultaneously, the Bureau became the Forest Service, the first agency of the federal government to have the word "service" in its title. In 1907 the reserves were re-named national forests.

Pinchot, the first chief of the Forest Service, remained in that post until 1910. He was a dynamic, inspiring leader who welded an organization out of young eastern forestry school graduates and western woodsmen—an organization marked for its esprit de corps down to this day. It would be difficult to assess the degree to which Pinchot's views and ideas influenced the equally dynamic Theodore Roosevelt. During the Roose-velt administrations, however, there was a marked expansion of the national forests and the groundwork was laid for their effective management. During that period, also, "conserva-tion" became a household word in the United States. Roose-velt's White House Conference of Governors, called in 1908, led to the appointment of the National Conservation Commis-sion whose report to Congress in 1909 was the first comprehen-sive inventory of United States resources—land, water, forest, and mineral. Thus federal activity in forestry served to spark a movement for the conservation of all resources.

Organizing the administration and management of the na-tional forests was the single largest forestry endeavor of the first decade of this century. It was not the only one however. By 1910 the states having organized forestry programs stood at 25. Eleven of these were administering 3 million acres of state-owned forest land. In 1910 a Forestry Division was es-tablished in the Office of Indian Affairs, Department of the Interior, to manage forest lands set aside for use of the Indians. Nevertheless, forestry was the province of the public agencies in this early period; cut out and get out still the practice of the lumber industry.

Simultaneously, with the development of forest conserva-tion activities, there came professional orientation and growth. In 1900 a group of seven foresters founded the Society of American Foresters. Its objectives were "To further the cause of forestry in America by fostering a spirit of comradeship among American foresters; by creating opportunities for a free interchange of views upon forestry and allied subjects; and by disseminating a knowledge of the purpose and achievements of forestry." With its objectives little changed today the Society has proved an effective force in promoting technical knowledge, advances in forest science and practice, and professional education and ideals.

1911 to World War I

The year 1911 is a milestone in forestry history. Congress enacted the Weeks Law, which opened the way to extension of the national forest system to the East by authorizing the federal government to purchase forest lands at the headwaters of navigable rivers. The value of forests in watershed protection was thus given official recognition. Moreover, the Weeks Law authorized the use of federal funds for cooperation with the states in the prevention and control of forest fires. The policy of federal-state cooperation in forestry—later greatly expanded—was thereby established and has subsequently played a major role in state forest-conservation progress.

Forestry research, which actually in its empirical sense preceded any action programs, had been formally undertaken by the Forest Service by the initiation of its regional experiment station program in 1908. Two years later the Forest Products Laboratory was established in Wisconsin. In 1915 a Branch of Research was organized, giving full recognition to the necessity for scientific research in the best means of managing forest land resources and utilizing their products and services.

The Effects of World War I

World War I sent many foresters into military service and many others into the production of wood products for the war effort here at home. Overseas the Twentieth Engineers (Forestry) was at one time the largest regiment in the American Expeditionary Force; its mission to produce wood products for the A.E.F. Most of its officers were American foresters and a large portion of its enlisted personnel skilled American loggers. The War, short though its span seems in retrospect, ended an era in forestry history in this country. A forestry profession had emerged, and many basic principles of forestry practices as adapted for the United States had been formulated. The practice of forestry on the ground was, however, almost entirely limited to the national forests, Indian lands, and some state forests.

Wartime demand for timber focused attention on the need to apply forestry principles to the private land that accounted for nearly three-fourths of the nation's commercial forests. Regulation by the government was proposed and arguments pro and con filled forestry- and lumber-trade journals. Then in 1920 a Senate Committee on Reforestation was appointed to study the matter. Its final recommendations left out controversial approaches and stressed those on which practically all foresters agreed. The result was passage of the Clarke-McNary Act of 1924, which, through cooperative measures among federal, state, and private groups, has been responsible for much of the progress made in state and private forestry efforts. This law expanded federal cooperation in fire protection, in production and distribution of planting stock, and in advising and assisting woodland owners. It provided for the cooperative employment of state extension foresters, who would educate woodland owners by demonstrating forestry in the woods. The law also extended the land-acquisition powers of the federal government under the Weeks Law to include land for timber production as well as navigable stream watershed protection.

Four years later, in 1928, the McSweeney-McNary Law increased federal funds for forestry research at the experiment stations and the Forest Products Laboratory. It also provided for an inventory of the nation's forest resources. Since 1930 the nationwide Forest Survey has been a continuing and major activity of the Forest Service.

By the end of the 1920's some 3,500 men technically trained in forestry were so engaged, largely in federal and state agencies. About 300 professional foresters were being graduated annually by some 20 colleges and universities. The results of research by the Forest Service, some states, and some of the schools were bringing about marked betterment in the techniques being applied to public forests. Advances in the technology of forest-fire control were especially significant. State forestry was expanding rapidly under the stimulus of federal-state cooperative programs. The basic concepts of multiple-use forest-land management were being evolved even to the extent that the Forest Service was giving some attention to setting aside wilderness areas in the national forests. In the previously cutover South, Lake States, and Northeast proximity to markets and other favorable circumstances were leading some of the more progressive forest industries to pioneer in the practice of forestry on their holdings during the 1920's. In the Pacific Northwest, to which the lumber industry had shifted its center, with its vast stands of virgin forest, there was yet little or no economic incentive to grow timber on private land. In the late 1920's the poor economic condition of the lumber industry was one of the first signs of the general depression to come.

The Depression

The years of the Great Depression strongly influenced forestry history. Even at their outset the ills of the lumber industry had prompted President Hoover to appoint a Timber Conservation Board in 1930 to study the situation. Before the Board could report, the general depression was here; and in 1932 the U.S. Senate called on the Secretary of Agriculture to draw up plans for a coordinated federal and state program for the utilization of forest lands. *A National Plan for American Forestry,* commonly called "The Copeland Report," was issued the following year. The report made extensive proposals for public and private programs, including greatly expanded public ownership.

Several public-works programs of the depression years had

direct forestry implications. The Civilian Conservation Corps was created in 1933 to provide work for needy youth and to build up the nation's natural resources. At its peak in 1935, of 2,600 camps, half were doing forestry projects. Many long-range improvements were made on national and state forest lands, useful employment was provided, and as an indirect benefit thousands of young men were indoctrinated with at least the basic precepts of forest conservation. The start of World War II in 1941 brought about the end of the program.

The newly created (1933) Soil Conservation Service stimulated farm woodland owners to plant trees and manage existing woodlots.

Forestry has played an important role in the history of accomplishments of the Tennessee Valley Authority, established in 1933 also.

Though the National Industrial Recovery Act (of 1933) was ruled unconstitutional two years later, Article X of the Act had lasting benefits. The article specified certain practices to be carried out by the lumber industry to leave cutover land in good condition. Several of the major industry associations established forestry committees in order to comply with the provisions of the Act and then continued them afterward in the form of committees and forestry departments that went on functioning.

The dust storms of the early 1930's brought about the Shelterbelt Program, first administered by the Forest Service, later by the Soil Conservation Service. More than 33,000 farmers in the plains states participated in planting over 18,000 miles of shelterbelts in the first seven years of the program after its initiation in 1934.

The acquisition of national forest land was much expanded in the 1930's in the South and in the Central and Lake States. Most of the acquisition was industry cutover lands.

In 1937 the Norris-Doxey Cooperative Farm Forestry Act was passed, increasing the slope and intensity of federal-state cooperation in aiding farm-woodland owners in growing and marketing timber. (The Act was later repealed, in 1950, in favor of the more inclusive Cooperative Forest Management Act.)

The same year Congress reversed its long-term policy of seeking the liquidation of land and timber on the Department of the Interior O. and C. lands in Oregon. These were lands originally reclaimed from forfeited railroad grants. In 1937 Congress provided for permanent retention of the some 2 million acres of O. and C. lands in federal ownership and for their management under a mandate requiring localized application of a sustained-yield policy.

The depression years focused attention on the results of forest devastation in many parts of the eastern United States—tax delinquency and the loss of jobs in wood-using industries. Public regulation was again widely discussed and subsequently several states adopted minimal regulatory measures.

But, perhaps strangely, the depression years saw in the South the start of what has been a major breakthrough in private forestry. With the establishment of new pulp and paper mills there an important market for trees of small size was developed. The industry began a steady growth that still continues.

World War II

The vastly accelerated demands for wood and wood products during the years of World War II had immediate and long-lasting effects. Of the immediate effects, the most striking was the volume production of the forest industries. In the East a Timber Production War Project by the Forest Service in cooperation with the War Production Board helped operators locate stumpage and secure needed supplies, equipment, and manpower. In the West dwindling private stumpage brought about a new reliance on national forest timber and a program of access-road building that opened up many previously isolated areas.

The war stimulated many improved uses for wood as well

as new ones. The war-caused shortages of forest products brought about a greatly increased public awareness of the economic importance of forestry, as well as an improved price structure for forest products that strongly influenced further advances in both the public and the private sector of forestry.

Problems and Progress of Recent Decades

Having explored in some detail the development of forest conservation in the United States up to the end of World War II, current history can be seen as an intensification and refinement of basic precepts previously established, along with the emergence of a much wider appreciation of the interdependence of all resources and of a vastly increased amount of forestry being practiced in the private sector.

Surveys. Immediately following the war both The American Forestry Association and the Forest Service made appraisals of the national forest resource though concerned with the impact of four years of war's demands. Based on its, and the Forest Service, findings, AFA called its Third American Forest Congress in 1946. At its fourth congress in 1953 AFA adopted a program for a national forest policy based on three primary goals: (1) to meet the essentials of forest protection, (2) to improve the national timber crop in volume and quality to a degree sufficient to wipe out all deficits and build up a reserve, and (3) to obtain the maximum of economic and social services from our forests by realistic application of the principle of multiple use in their management.

Following a study in cooperation with the states and private industry the Forest Service in 1958 published its revised Timber Resources Review under the title of *Timber Resources for America's Future.* The report presented data on growth, drain, and demand for forest products. It projected needs for 1975 and the year 2000. It stressed the need for intensified forestry practices on all lands to meet anticipated needs by the end of the twentieth century. Again in 1965 the Forest Service updated its evaluation of the forest estate in *Timber Trends in the United States.* This report notes improvement in the growth-drain (harvest and mortality from fire, insects, and disease) relationship, but notes also declining quality of available supplies and again warns of later shortages unless intensive forestry practices are applied to all public and private lands.

Private Forestry. One of the most important areas of progress in the past twenty years has been the upsurge of intensive forestry practiced on industrially owned timberlands. This progress has been made possible by the demand for products and the resultant favorable economic climate, and to the rapid expansion of the pulp-and-paper industry, notably in the South. In 1965 industry is estimated to employ one-third of all professional foresters in the country.

On the other hand, 59 per cent of the commercial forest land of the contiguous United States is in farms and other non-industrial ownership. It is primarily to these lands, rather than those in public or industrial ownership, that we must look for the major improvement in management practices that will raise the level of production in volume and quality to the level predicted as needed in the year 2000.

Following an unsuccessful attempt to again raise the issue of public regulation of private timber land, the role of the federal government as a cooperator with state and private forestry programs was firmly established by passage in 1950 of the Cooperative Forest Management Act. This replaced the Norris-Doxey Act and extended federal-state cooperative-management aid to all forest landowners, and made technical advice and assistance available to forest-products processors. The stimulus to fire protection and tree planting on private lands stemming from the results of the Clarke-McNary Act of 1924 has been very great. The provisions of both of these Acts are financed jointly by the federal government and the individual states. The Forest Service, representing the government, oversees the expenditure of federal funds and lends a measure of guidance, but it is the state-forestry agency that actually administers the programs of assistance to private owners.

The result of the two Acts has been an impressive and

firmly grounded growth in state forestry programs, which in 1963 had an annual total budget of $119,476,000. The National Association of State Foresters reports that most of the increase came from state appropriations, indicating growing state concern with forest conservation. In 1963 the states employed over 2,000 professionally educated foresters and owned over 19 million acres of forest land.

Protection. Through the use of aircraft, radio communication, and mechanized equipment, fire control has progressed to the point that insects and disease cause greater annual losses. More than 90 per cent of the forest-land area of the United States is under some degree of protection. Nevertheless, fires take their annual toll, and their control is the major annual cost of protecting the resource.

The Forest Pest Control Act, passed by Congress in 1947, authorizes federal cooperation in the control of forest pests and tree diseases.

The National Forests. As of June 30, 1963, there were 154 national forests located in 39 states and Puerto Rico. Their total area was approximately 182 million acres.

In calendar year 1964 these forests supplied: 11 billion board feet of timber; grazing for 6 million head of domestic livestock; and had 134 million recreation visitors.

The most marked development in recent years concerning the national forests is increased use. The annual cut has gone up steadily and recreation use has risen astronomically, with its attendant problems. Indicative of the increasing role of the national forests in our day-to-day national life have been two Congressional Acts of recent years. It speaks well of the foresight of the Forest Service that both Acts simply gave Congressional sanction to policies and programs of long standing. In 1960 the Multiple Use Act directed that the national forests should be managed for the production and use of all their goods and services—wood, water, forage, wildlife, and recreation.

In 1964 Public Law 88577, after several years of debate and

frequent amendment of the "Wilderness Bill," established the National Wilderness Preservation System. Although the law provides for the probable future inclusion of other lands, the system at original establishment consists of 9.1 million acres in 54 units on national forests. This land had in the past been designated as wilderness and so managed and protected by the Forest Service.

Other Federal Lands. The Bureau of Land Management, formed in 1946 by combining the General Land Office and the Grazing Service in the Department of the Interior, administers the public domain lands under policies generally similar to those applied by the Forest Service to the national forests. Its principal forestry functions concern sustained-yield management of the O. and C. lands and fire protection in interior Alaska.

The Bureau of Indian Affairs manages 6.6 million acres of commercial forest on behalf of the American Indians out of a total of 56 million acres owned by or dedicated to Indian use.

Forested lands of the national parks, while not supporting commercial timber harvesting, must be protected from fire, insects, disease, and human vandalism. Increasing hoards of visitors pose difficult problems in preserving many areas in their natural-forest condition.

Military reservations in the United States total some 32 million acres. Some of the reservations contain substantial areas of forest. In recent years the Department of Defense has adopted a policy of applying good-conservation practices to the land, consistent with military use. The Department has sought the aid of the Forest Service and other federal agencies in developing management plans and has added foresters and wildlife managers to its civilian staff.

Some 340,000 acres of forest land surrounding Tennessee Valley Authority reservoirs are managed under sound forestry principles for demonstration purposes, timber production, watershed protection, and recreation.

Professional Education. Forty-four colleges and universities in the United States offered instruction leading to the undergraduate degree in forestry in 1964. In that year enrollment was at an all-time high of 9,412 undergraduates. The schools awarded 1,599 undergraduate degrees, 347 master degrees, and 86 doctor degrees. Of the undergraduate degrees, 1,097 were in general forestry, while the remainder were in wood technology, range management, wildlife management, forest recreation, and miscellaneous. Of the total enrollment 70 were women students.

An estimated 21,000 professionally educated foresters were engaged in forestry or allied work in 1964. It was further estimated that 50 per cent of these were in public employ, 37 per cent in private, 6 per cent in education, and 7 per cent in miscellaneous employ.

The Challenge

In his introductory chapter to the book *American Forestry: Six Decades of Growth* (Society of American Foresters, 1960) Yale School of Forestry Dean George Garratt closes with a prophetic warning that becomes less prophetic with each passing year:

Today, as in the past, conflict over land use lies at the root of many problems in American Conservation. The conflict has been heightened in recent years by pressures for exclusive permanent use of forest land for extended park systems and wilderness areas, reservoirs and flood control dams, urban and industrial developments, and various other purposes, all in the face of increasing requirements for timber production and other multiple uses. Not yet apparent, but of high future significance, is the prospect of conversion to cropland and pasture of large areas of the more productive forest lands, to meet the food and forage requirements of our rapidly growing population. The magnitude of the potential withdrawals of land now in timber production may well threaten the raw material base of the wood-using industries in the not-so distant future.

For Further Reading

CLEPPER, HENRY, and MEYER, ARTHUR B. *American Forestry: Six Decades of Growth.* Society of American Foresters, Washington, D.C. 1960.

DANA, SAMUEL TRASK. *Forest and Range Policy: Its Development in the United States.* McGraw-Hill Book Co., Inc., New York. 1956.

FOREST SERVICE, U.S. DEPARTMENT OF AGRICULTURE. *Timber Trends in the United States.* Superintendent of Documents, U.S. Government Printing Office, Washington, D.C. 1965.

FRANK, BERNARD. *Our National Forests.* University of Oklahoma Press, Norman, Okla. 1955.

FROME, MICHAEL. *Whose Woods These Are: The Story of the National Forests.* Doubleday & Co., Inc., Garden City, N.Y. 1962.

GREELEY, WILLIAM B. *Forest Policy.* McGraw-Hill Book Co., Inc., New York. 1953.

ISE, JOHN. *The United States Forest Policy.* Yale University Press, New Haven, Conn. 1920.

POMEROY, KENNETH B. *The Job Ahead: Proceedings of the Fifth American Forestry Congress.* The American Forestry Association, Washington, D.C. 1964.

CHAPTER FOUR

FISHERIES AND AQUATIC RESOURCES

Lakes, Streams, and Other Inland Waters

Richard H. Stroud

The early European immigrants came to America seeking a new world free of old oppressions. One oppression was a preferential reservation of fishing rights to the landed gentry. Consequently, upon settling in America, the immigrants established in the colonial statutes the revolutionary new concept of common rights of ownership to the fish and game resources. Custody of these resources was vested in the government as a public trust. This principle has remained essentially unchanged to the present.

Within a few short decades after their arrival, the settlers by forest destruction had upset the North American ecological environment, of which the Indians were a part, that had characterized the continent for centuries. An early incentive to accelerated land-clearing was an almost insatiable demand in Europe for tobacco. The colonial planters worked feverishly to clear vast new areas annually to keep up with demand.

The colonists constructed grist mills, dammed and polluted waterways, and harvested anadromous fish runs relentlessly. Soon, the combined effects had eliminated the Atlantic salmon from the rivers south of the St. Lawrence in Canada. Atlantic shad were reduced in abundance as well. Brook trout, orig-

R. WILLIAM ESCHMEYER

1905–1955

Popularizer of Fisheries Management

inally abundant, became extirpated from many waters as a corollary of forest destruction.

It early became evident that fishery resources were dwindling, but the reasons were not understood. Even so, the first closed season was enacted in Massachusetts in 1652. As the settlers pushed inland and fishery stocks dwindled, they frequently imposed simple kinds of harvesting restrictions that they hoped might help but seldom did.

By the middle decades of the eighteenth century, a few European naturalists had begun making sporadic fish collections in the New World. A number of descriptive reports resulted, with those of Peter Artedi having influenced Linnaeus' *magnus opus* on biological classification, Systema Naturae. The heyday of American ichthyology awaited the arrival over a century later at Harvard University of Louis Agassiz. Agassiz's enthusiasm stimulated the ichthyological interests of several budding scientists including David Starr Jordan, America's greatest ichthyologist.

During the final decades of the nineteenth century, under Jordan's leadership, American ichthyology came into its golden era of collection, description, and classification of American fishes. It culminated in Jordan's publication (with Barton Warren Evermann) of the monumental four-volume *Fishes of North and Middle America* (1896–1900). This was followed by Jordan and Evermann's popular treatise, *American Food and Game Fishes* (1902).

Jordan's continuing influence, through his numerous students, remains of major significance in shaping American fish conservation. Although many details remain to be studied, most inland fishes are now described and their relationships sufficiently understood for dependable use by the viable new breed of modern fishery biologists who have developed a dynamic philosophy of fish conservation. Current progress in refining taxonomic details is recorded in *Copeia*, the journal of the American Society of Ichthyology and Herpetology; the Society was organized in 1916, and the journal's current format was adopted in 1930.

Early Governmental Actions

During the latter half of the nineteenth century, there arose demands that government "do something" to preserve fish. These led to establishment of administrative mechanisms—the precursors of present-day conservation departments—for enforcing restrictive measures and to propagate fish for stocking depleted waters. There was early recognition of state prerogatives in such matters as legal jurisdiction over the fishery resources. The first government fishery agencies were created in Massachusetts in 1856, in New Hampshire and Vermont in 1865, and in other states rapidly thereafter. Fishing licenses soon followed as a means of financing the activities of the new agencies.

In 1871 Congress established the U.S. Fish Commission to "look into the cause of depletion" and otherwise aid the fisheries. Assigned a research function, the new commission nevertheless began an extensive program of artificial propagation, unabated to this day. From the start, under Commissioner Spencer F. Baird (a naturalist), the commission's activities considerably influenced policy among state fishery organizations. Its latter-day counterpart is the U.S. Fish and Wildlife Service (combining the bureaus of Sport Fisheries and Wildlife and of Commercial Fisheries), which exercises an essentially partnership role with the states.

Until the middle of the eighteenth century nothing new was learned about methods of propagating fish that had not been recorded by the Chinese many centuries before Christ. In 1741, Ludwig Jacobi of Westphalia, Germany, was able to repeat the fertilization of trout eggs artificially. Nearly a century later, the method of artificial insemination of fish eggs was rediscovered by two illiterate French fishermen. A French biology professor described their activities in 1849 and established the first fish-breeding station at Hünigen in 1850. The success achieved led scientists and public alike to believe that man had cleverly improved upon nature. The resulting enthu-

siasm for artificial fish propagation that swept over Europe
and North America scarcely began to abate by mid-twentieth
century!

The first state fish commission (Massachusetts) had been
established in order to apply the new procedures to stock public waters. The U.S. Fish Commission engaged in a program
of interchanging various species between East and West and
importing Old World species. In 1871 some 35,000 fertilized
Atlantic shad eggs were shipped from New York's Hudson
River to California's Sacramento River. In 1873 the Commission shipped 2 million fertilized chinook salmon eggs from the
West Coast to eastern waters without success. Two plants
totaling 432 fingerling striped bass, from New Jersey's Navesink
River, were made in San Francisco Bay and Suisun Bay in 1879
and 1882. Striped bass became abundant throughout the Bay
area within a decade. Many other similar efforts were unsuccessful, but western rainbow trout were successfully inter-
changed with eastern brook trout. (In mid-twentieth century,
remarkably successful imaginative introductions of selected
saltwater species into the Salton Sea, including Corvina, were
made by California biologists.) The introduction and nationwide distribution of the ubiquitous carp, carried out with state
encouragement by the U.S. Fish Commission between 1878
and 1886, was a major blunder. In American waters its feeding habits served, by roiling the water, to destroy the suita-
bility of habitat for native game and food species. Brown
trout were a far more propitious introduction, although its
detractors are many. (In mid-twentieth century, successful
introduction of *Tilapia* from North Africa for controlled use
in southern waters was quite different from the unresearched
introduction of carp in the previous century.)

In 1897 the U.S. Fish Commission issued its important
Manual of Fish Culture, which went through several revisions
until 1905. For several decades it was the definitive work on
classical fish culture. Recent technological advances have augmented the basic methods developed by the pioneer culturists
who compiled the *Manual*, especially concerning use of light

and hormones to regulate spawning and formulation of dry-pelletted fortified feeds.

Scientific Collaboration

The existence of hundreds of fish-culture stations led to the formation in 1870 of the American Fish Culture Association (renamed the American Fisheries Society in 1884) to "advance a correct knowledge of the best theory and practice of the science of fish culture." The American Fisheries Society antedates all other specialized groups in natural science or conservation, and it is the principal society for fishery scientists. The majority of its members are biologists engaged in research or management of America's fishery resources. The organization's official publication is the *Transactions of the American Fisheries Society*, published without interruption since 1870. This quarterly scientific journal is the principal repository for significant technical reports on fishery-related subjects, including pollution, limnology, oceanography, ichthyology, fish culture, fishery management, nutrition, fishery biology, and parasitology.

The early decades of the twentieth century witnessed the birth and early nourishment of the conservation movement as a new philosophy. In those few decades the general public was imbued with a new consciousness that renewable natural resources must be scientifically husbanded to provide for maximum sustained yields, and thus public use without harm to future supply. The relationships of fish conservation with forest, water, soil, and wildlife conservation were established. The dawn of the twentieth century also heralded the matriculation of a needed new ecological emphasis in study of inland fishery resources. The eventual accumulation from these beginnings of a stockpile of biological facts about the life-histories and ecology of a number of game and forage species, and the gradual appreciation of controlling limnological influences, furnished scientists with provocative insights into behavior patterns and population dynamics of fishes.

In 1918 a monumental work by Henry B. Ward and George C. Whipple, *Fresh-Water Biology*, was published with the collaboration of a staff of 25 specialists in biology, botany, zoology, and limnology. That work stood without peer until the publication, in 1953, of *Fresh-Water Invertebrates of the United States*, by Robert W. Pennak of the University of Colorado. Together with a remarkable series of monographs on aquatic insects that emanated from the Illinois Natural History Survey, some notable contributions on aquatic invertebrates by James G. Needham at Cornell University, a veritable torrent of limnological papers by E. A. Birge and C. E. Juday at the University of Wisconsin, there developed a broad basis of understanding of the aquatic environment of fishes that was a vital prerequisite to emergence of new concepts of fish conservation. In 1935 Paul S. Welch of the University of Michigan synthesized the elements of a broad and diverse literature on the aquatic habitat in *Limnology*, a textbook that has since helped to train an entire generation of fishery biologists. It is noteworthy that the Limnological Society of America (now the Society of Limnology and Oceanography) was formed one year earlier to provide an organization and scientific journal for this lusty new science. Not until 1957, when G. Evelyn Hutchinson of Yale University published the first of a planned two-volume reference, *A Treatise on Limnology*, was the pre-eminence of Welch's *Limnology* threatened.

Among the more noteworthy early studies of statewide aquatic resources were those of the Illinois Natural History Survey that produced the classic monograph, *The Fishes of Illinois* (1908; revised 1920), by Stephen A. Forbes and Robert E. Richardson. Several other important state fish surveys followed. Representative of a more intensive kind of study was another classical monograph, *The Ecology and Economics of Oneida Lake Fish* (1928), by Charles C. Adams and Thomas L. Hankinson of Syracuse University.

During the early 1900's interest had developed in studying the life-histories and ecology of fishes and the limnology of their aquatic habitats. Centers for this new fishery biology developed at Cornell University under George C. Embody; at the University of Michigan under Carl L. Hubbs; at the Illinois Natural History Survey under Stephen A. Forbes; at the University of Minnesota under Samuel Eddy (later, under Lloyd L. Smith, Jr.); at the University of Wisconsin under E. A. Birge; at the University of Toronto (Ontario) under James R. Dymond; and at others. Students and young associates trained at these centers fanned out over North America and exerted a profound influence upon the development of modern fish conservation. In 1965, 106 universities and colleges offered undergraduate or graduate courses in fishery biology, ichthyology, hydrobiology, or limnology. They include 16 universities where Federal-State Cooperative Fishery Units had been established. A total of 422 professors was engaged in teaching and research in the fishery field at those institutions.

One of the important university contributions in the 1920's was the validation of the scale method of age-and-growth analysis for several species of American fishes following discovery of the method by European biologists. American pioneers in these critical studies included A. G. Huntsman of the University of Toronto, John Van Oosten of the U.S. Bureau of Fisheries (whitefishes), Ralph Hile of the U.S. Bureau of Fisheries (cisco; rock bass); and several University of Michigan graduate students, including Charles W. Creaser (sunfish), Frank W. Jobes (yellow perch), and H. J. Deason (pike-perches). European biologists had applied the scale method to salmon and trout two decades earlier. Scale analysis has since become a standard tool of the fishery manager, well reflected by several hundred papers listed in the *Handbook of Freshwater Biology*, compiled in 1950 (supplemented in 1953) by Kenneth D. Carlander of Iowa State University.

Conservation Accelerated

Following World War I, America's anglers became increasingly concerned over declining fishery resources. They were inspired to have outlawed the interstate shipment of illegally taken "black bass." The Federal Black Bass Act of 1926 (amended to include other species in 1930 and 1947) was milestone conservation legislation, serving to eradicate commercial fishing for game fishes. Anglers were equally concerned over widespread pollution of America's waterways. Even though rivers have great capacity for biological assimilation of pollutants, fish populations had dwindled near urban centers and fishermen correctly discerned a cause-and-effect relationship. By the early 1930's the Izaak Walton League of America was well organized and fighting to free waterways of the pollution blight. In 1948 its crusade was rewarded by enactment of a temporary federal water-pollution-control law (extended in 1958).

Big dams were blamed in the postwar period for major destruction of fishery resources. Based upon arbitrary assumptions, conservationists condemned all such dams indiscriminately. The view was generally sound where anadromous species, such as salmon and steelhead trout, were affected. However, research on warmwater fishes in Tennessee Valley Authority reservoirs, in the 1930's and 1940's, would demonstrate a need for discrimination otherwise. The big-dam controversy caused passage of sportsmen-sponsored federal legislation (1934; amended in 1946, 1948, and 1958) known since 1958 as the Fish and Wildlife Coordination Act. It authorized river-basins studies to evaluate effects of water projects on fish and wildlife and recommend appropriate corrective actions. It caused studies of means for anadromous fishes, such as Pacific salmon and steelhead trout, to bypass dams and led to incorporation of fish screens, fish ladders, hatcheries, and other devices, as well as modifications in procedures for handling water flows, as integral parts of water developments.

Many thoughtful anglers had long since begun to realize that much traditional regulation and indiscriminate fish stocking were arbitrary. Their questioning made politically appointed administrators uneasy and caused them to hire university fish "experts" to conduct summertime biological surveys of lakes and streams—the first resource inventories by biologists. The first full-time fishery biologist was employed in 1923 by the Michigan Department of Conservation. By the mid-1930's a number of the larger states had also employed a few fishery biologists full time.

Advances in Research

In 1930 the Institute for Fisheries Research was organized at the University of Michigan under Carl L. Hubbs, a former student of Jordan, with succeeding direction by Albert S. Hazzard (followed by Gerald P. Cooper). The work and ideas of Hubbs, his students, and his associates inspired future programs throughout America. Some of the more imaginative biologists were commencing to recognize that they were dealing with diverse natural laws, forces, and interactions that could be analyzed and correlated into a basis for intelligent action.

Between the wars—the spawning period for modern fish conservation—Hubbs borrowed rotenone from the South American Indians and first employed it (with Milton Trautman) in the United States in 1934 to eradicate stunted perch from a small Michigan pond. Use of rotenone has since developed into one of the professional fish conservationist's most sophisticated management tools, with up to 100,000 acres of poor fishing waters being chemically rehabilitated each year.

Hubbs turned the attention and energies of the Michigan Institute at an early date to the matter of habitat improvement. The Institute's first management bulletin, prepared in 1932 by Hubbs and two of his students (John R. Greeley and Clarence M. Tarzwell), dealt with *Methods for the Improvement of Michigan Trout Streams*. The second, prepared in 1938 by Hubbs and another student (R. William Eschmeyer), concerned *The Improvement of Lakes for Fishing*. These two documents established habitat improvement as a permanent element of fish conservation, despite later emergence of decided limitations. One of the studies conducted under Hubbs' direction concerned warmwater-fish spawning at Deep Lake,

Michigan, by William F. Carbine. The findings (that normal fry production averaged over a half-million per acre) eventually sealed the fate of promiscuous maintenance stocking of warmwater fish, although many states continued the practice until after World War II.

At Cornell University, George C. Embody stimulated the development of fish culture through his noted lectures and graduate students. In addition, his ideas on lake and stream surveys generated widespread evaluations of traditional fish-stocking practices. One of Embody's students, Karl F. Lagler, migrated to the University of Michigan where he commenced to train part of another generation of fishery students. In 1952 Lagler published the first of the modern fishery textbooks, *Freshwater Fishery Biology.*

At Cortland, New York, in 1932, C. M. McCay established a cooperative state-federal trout-nutrition laboratory. His nutritional research, and that of A. V. Tunison in particular, since continued by Arthur M. Phillips, has strongly affected hatchery procedures. These were further affected by H. S. Davis' definitive studies on fish diseases, extended later by Stanislaus Snieszko at a federal experimental hatchery at Leetown, West Virginia.

During the 1940's, the Michigan Institute under Albert S. Hazzard (with biologists Justin W. Leonard, David S. Shetter, and others) turned its attentions to problems of trout-stream-fishery management. It became quickly evident that resident trout populations can supply comparatively few fish for harvest on a sustained-yield basis. Consequently, in the 1950's and 1960's, Hazzard was to urge application of catch-and-release (no-harvest) regulations, on the better-quality heavily fished trout streams, as a means of circumventing characteristically low natural production of trout that has stimulated stocking with catchable-size hatchery trout. Essentially a high size-limit regulation, catch-and-release required use of artificial lures that hooking mortality studies had shown are less destructive of released trout than use of natural bait. Touted as a new panacea by special-interest trouting groups, organized to promote this "Hazzard Plan" for trout management, continuing scientific assessment revealed serious flaws. At least one clear consequence is discouragement of fishing use except by fly-fishing purists. Farther north, F. E. J. Fry and his associates at the University of Toronto conducted physiological studies on trout metabolism and environmental requirements. D. S. Rawson, University of Saskatchewan, predicted fish yields in large northern Canadian lakes, utilizing sophisticated limnological analyses. Richard B. Miller at the University of Alberta conducted replicated field studies on mortality of stocked hatchery trout in the presence and absence of resident trout. His findings caused major revisions of hatchery procedures.

About the time that reservoir research was commencing (early 1930's) at the Tennessee Valley Authority—to which Eschmeyer brought his special talents a few years later—other research was unfolding both in the North and in the South. At the rejuvenated Illinois Natural History Survey, George W. Bennett was initiating experimental management of small, artificial fishing lakes. At what is now Auburn University, in Alabama, an imaginative entomologist named Homer S. Swingle and an ecologically minded botanist named E. V. Smith were teaming up at an experimental farm-ponds laboratory of unprecedented scope that was destined to achieve world renown within two decades.

Bennett's intensive research revealed the fallacy of oft-repeated arbitrary contentions that declining productivity is an inevitable consequence of impoundment. He showed substantial benefits to warmwater-game-fish production from controlled drawdown of water levels. Eventually (in 1962), Bennett collated his twenty-five years of pioneering research with other significant findings in his comprehensive *Management of Artificial Lakes and Ponds*. Swingle and his associates undertook many hundreds of controlled and replicated paired-pond experiments evaluating various species combinations, stocking rates, fertilizer applications, and artificial feeding in terms of standing crops, population composition, and continuous sustained-fishing yields for food and for sport. Highly sophisticated pond-fish-management procedures resulted that gave impetus, under promotion by the U.S. Soil Conservation Service, to construction of nearly 2 million farm ponds. Applicability to fishery management in small impoundments (up to several hundred surface acres) of the principles that Swingle enunciated (1950) in his notable *Relationships and Dynamics of Balanced and Unbalanced Fish Populations* has been abundantly demonstrated. Outstanding fishing attesting to this has been created and maintained since 1950 by the Alabama Conservation Department in nearly 20 public-fishing lakes, comprising nearly 2,000 acres, annually supporting 100 to 300 angler-days of fishing per acre.

Meanwhile, intensive year-round studies of anglers' harvests, game-fish populations, fish-food organisms, age and growth of fishers, and limnological characteristics of TVA reservoirs afforded exciting new insights into the dynamics of reservoir biology. These studies, by Eschmeyer and his associates, generated a revolutionary new concept of year-round fishing (including spring fishing) for warmwater game fishes. It was first applied, in 1944, to Norris Reservoir, Tennessee, without prejudice to maintenance of fish populations but with subsequent doubling of fishing opportunity and fish harvest. By another decade, two-thirds of the states had similarly liberalized their fishing regulations for warmwater species, the first two states (simultaneously in 1945) having been Ohio— where E. L. Wickliff, Lee S. Roach, and others had long pondered the significance of their own provocative fish-population data—and Nebraska. In addition to liberalization of fishing regulations, conceived by Eschmeyer, the existing concept of controlling food-competitive (non-game) fishes to encourage game-fish production was strengthened at TVA, especially from the research by Tarzwell. Commercial fishing for nongame fishes was encouraged.

In Washington there commenced a remarkable combination of studies by Robert C. Meigs and Clarence F. Pautzke on the life-history of the anadromous steelhead trout and at the Tacoma state hatchery on rearing of steelhead fingerlings within one season to downstream-migratory size for planting. This at least partly circumvented critical natural factors controlling natural steelhead production within spawning streams (bypassing the normal two-year nursery-stream residency required to reach critical downstream-migratory size). The new procedures applied by Pautzke (who later became Commissioner, U.S. Fish and Wildlife Service) and his associates eventually resulted in substantial increases in the number of adult steelheads returning from the sea to their "parent" hatchery streams—and in recreational fishing, the ultimate goal.

New Directions and Programs

In 1949, feeling a responsibility to aid in conserving fishery resources, the fishing-tackle industry organized the Sport Fishing Institute. Arthur R. Benson, an outstanding conservationist, was elected president. He held the office for nearly a decade until succeeded by Henry G. Shakespeare, another noted conservationist. R. W. Eschmeyer was invited to direct the Institute and coordinate nationwide fish-conservation activities, while defining and stimulating needed new activities. Eschmeyer was succeeded, upon his sudden death in 1955, by Richard H. Stroud, former research assistant to Eschmeyer at TVA. Through a program of research in fishery biology, fish-conservation education of lay conservationists, and professional service to key conservation groups, the Institute plays a significant role as a catalyst for national policy formulation and for rapid development of effective state-action programs leading to improved sport fishing. By 1965, too, the Institute had awarded 142 graduate fellowships or research grants in fishery biology at 44 universities and colleges, thereby helping to train 83 fishery scientists. In 1963 Stroud and others organized the Sport Fishery Research Foundation, designed to augment availability of graduate fishery-research fellowships and accelerate training of needed new fishery scientists at selected universities. Benson, now an elder statesman of conservation, was elected as the Foundation's first president.

Passage of the Dingell-Johnson Act (1950), authorizing a federal-aid program of fish restoration, provided the needed incentive to bring all states into the modern fish-conservation picture. The first federal administrator of the D-J program was John S. Gottschalk, later to become director of the U.S. Bureau of Sport Fisheries and Wildlife (1964). Gottschalk was a former student at Indiana University of William Ricker, who contributed greatly to the theory of fish-population dynamics. All state conservation departments quickly added fishery biologists to their staffs to devise and conduct qualifying fishery-research-and-management projects. The D-J program spearheaded a great burst of nationwide activity in research on various management-oriented biological problems, construction of hundreds of community-fishing lakes, acquisition and development of public access to millions of acres of previously inaccessible waters, chemical restoration to productive use of many hundred thousand acres of poor fishing waters, improved hatchery and stocking methodology, and simplified many arbitrary regulations without harm to future supply. A few state agencies were able for the first time to initiate management-oriented investigations of estuarine sport fisheries in the neglected "no-man's" brackish zone between strictly fresh and strictly salt water, for many species embracing critical low-salinity nursery areas. These were not the first estuarine studies, but the D-J program generated accelerated activity on the fishery resources of these important "border" waters. Striped bass received especially concentrated attention on both coasts. Presence of several important estuaries on the Atlantic Coast led to coordinated efforts by corresponding states, supervised by Edward C. Raney of Cornell University, to clarify population relationships.

In the mid-1950's, controversy arose over the role of the U.S. Fish and Wildlife Service in solving international problems affecting declining oceanic commercial fisheries. The resulting federal "Fish and Wildlife Act of 1956" effected a partial cleavage of the Service into the semi-independent Bureau of Sport Fisheries and Wildlife and Bureau of Commercial Fisheries. A Fish and Wildlife Commissioner coordinated activities of the two bureaus under a new Assistant Secretary of the Interior. Under prodding by the Sport Fishing Institute, a reservoir-fishery-research program was commenced under the new authority together with (upon passage of special authorization) a marine-game-fish-research program within Sport Fisheries and Wildlife. The Commercial Fisheries Bureau undertook an ambitious program of research and management (under James W. Moffett and associates) to control parasitic sea lampreys that had invaded the Great Lakes, via the Welland Canal at Niagara Falls, and to rehabilitate the devastated lake-trout populations.

Research by many contemporary biologists is accelerating, and revolutionary new conceptual breakthroughs may be expected. The relative significance of numerous current contributions must be left to the hindsight of the future. The sound concepts and useful approaches characterizing modern fish conservation by the mid-1960's were formally reflected in a declaration of policy unanimously adopted by the American Fisheries Society in 1964. Its *North American Fish Policy* represents the results of two years of active deliberation and formulation by the Society's select Fish Policy Committee. Including Albert S. Hazzard as chairman, that group of professional fish conservationists comprised A. D. Aldrich, David K. Caldwell, George E. Couldwell, W. Harry Everhart, Raymond E. Johnson, Ernest A. Lachner, Justin W. Leonard, Paul R. Needham, A. L. Pritchard, George A. Rounsefell, William F. Royce, and Richard H. Stroud.

For Further Reading

DAVISON, VERNE E. *Homemade Fishing*. The Stackpole Co., Harrisburg, Pa. 1953.

ESCHMEYER, R. W., and FICHTER, GEORGE S. *Good Fishing*. Harper & Row, Inc., New York. 1959.

MILLER, RICHARD B. *A Cool Curving World*. Longmans, Green & Co., Ltd., Toronto, Canada. 1962.

NETBOY, ANTHONY. *Salmon of the Pacific Northwest—Fish vs. Dams.* Binfords & Mort, Portland, Ore. 1958.

REID, GEORGE K. *Ecology of Inland Waters and Estuaries.* Reinhold Publishing Corp., New York. 1961.

ROUNSEFELL, GEORGE A., and EVERHART, W. HARRY. *Fishery Science—Its Methods and Application.* John Wiley & Sons, Inc., New York. 1953.

STROUD, RICHARD H. *Fish Conservation.* In *The Fisherman's Encyclopedia* (I. N. Gabrielson, ed.). The Stackpole Co., Harrisburg, Pa. 1963.

Coastal and Marine Waters

Clarence P. Idyll

Marine fish were the first natural resource of America to be exploited; the fisheries, the first industry. The exploitation of this resource began long before the settlement of North America, even before the "discovery" of the continent by Columbus. The great stocks of fish of the Grand Banks and the waters of Newfoundland were fished by vessels from Europe at least one hundred years before the exploring voyage of Cabot in 1497. In a report of his discoveries Cabot said, "There are plenty of fish—especially—of that kind which the savages call Baccalaos." This is the name of the cod in Basque, and the implication is strong that European fishermen had taught it to the American Indians. By the end of the sixteenth century more than two hundred vessels from France, Portugal, and England were fishing off American shores.

The existence of the fish resource had great influence on settlement. Shore bases for the support of fisheries were the nuclei of permanent communities along the coast of what is now New England. Wealth derived from the fisheries made the area prosper despite its rocky soil. Fishing was followed by trade, manufacturing, wealth, power, and culture; the pattern of life in the colonial era was established by the fisheries.

European nations, including England, France, Spain, and Portugal, salted cod aboard their vessels. For American colonists, salted cod was the main commodity of commerce in the famous triangle trade with the West Indies and Europe, exchanging cod for rum and sugar in the Caribbean Islands, and these products for currency and manufactured goods in Europe.

Later, in the eighteenth and nineteenth centuries, whaling was developed. A little before the middle of the nineteenth century some 680 boats sailed from New Bedford, Nantucket, and other New England ports to the Antarctic and Pacific Oceans, building great fortunes for their owners and leaving a permanent mark on the culture of the American society. In the Gulf of Mexico fisheries such as those for snapper and sea trout developed. On the Pacific Coast the two major species were salmon and halibut. The Alaska salmon canning industry started in 1878. The halibut fishery emerged as a major industry in the 1880's under the impetus of the completion of the cross-continental railroads, which opened the eastern markets.

When it became more difficult to catch fish, especially on grounds near shore, depletion was feared and fishermen carried their concern to the government. Restrictive legislation was imposed, as in Massachusetts, where, from 1623 to 1857, 359 legislative Acts were passed restricting fishing in various ways; other colonies acted in the same manner. It is likely, in hindsight, that most of the fish stocks were not depleted, and the restrictive measures applied to the activities of fishermen served only to lower their efficiency and raise the price of their product.

U.S. Fish Commission

In the nineteenth century, it was clear, whether depletion was a fact or not, that little understanding existed of the biology of exploited fishes, and variations in their abundance. This resulted, in 1871, in the creation of the U.S. Fish Commission. The first Commissioner, Spencer Fullerton Baird, was a fortunate choice, since he possessed remarkable personal qualities. Baird was a sound scientist and an effective leader, and he established the bureau on a firm foundation.

Convinced of an alarming decrease in the abundance of commercially important fishes, Baird focused the study of marine biology on the problems of the fisheries. The studies he initiated included fish culture, the taxonomy and distribution of fishes and related marine animals, their reproduction and movements, the ecology of sea-bottom communities, the parasites and diseases of fishes. He put these studies on a sound basis, laying the foundation for the new science of fishery biology in America. And his persuasiveness with Congressional committees and the public made this program acceptable—something many other fishery workers who have followed him have not been able to achieve even with equally meritorious programs.

Baird selected Woods Hole, on Cape Cod, as the location for the headquarters of the Commission's scientific effort. The laboratory, constructed in 1875, was the best equipped for its purpose in the world at that time. Johns Hopkins and Princeton Universities and Williams College all contributed funds to help buy the land for the new laboratory, with the understanding that they would have perpetual use of work space for a member of their faculty. Alexander Agassiz was a distinguished private donor.

Several of Spencer Baird's assistants contributed significantly to the progress of American conservation. The first of these, Theodore N. Gill, was a well-known ichthyologist. He prepared a comprehensive and intelligent plan of study of the fishes of commercial interest, and the effect of fishing on their stocks, and this formed the basis of the early research of the Commission. A. E. Verrill of Yale University assumed responsibility for the studies of invertebrates. George Brown Goode, who succeeded Baird as Commissioner of Fisheries on the death of the latter in 1884, prepared a comprehensive survey of the fisheries, as part of the 1880 Census.

In 1882 the Fish Commission vessel "Albatross" was put into service, and in the next two decades she traveled thousands of miles over the oceans of the world, performing notable work in the service of marine biology and the fisheries. Alexander Agassiz was in charge of much of this work.

In laying the foundations for conservation of America's

marine-fish resources, Spencer Baird was concerned, as nearly all fishery scientists have been, that most measures of the government were suppressive—at times so extreme as to shackle the fisherman in his efforts to exploit the stocks effectively. Anxious to find some positive measures that would create bigger catches, rather than negative rules that served only to reduce production, he was an enthusiastic supporter of fish culture, as one positive kind of program.

Baird was supported in this view by the general opinion of his time. The consequence was that great emphasis was placed on fish culture in the early work of the Fish Commission. In 1885 the "Fish Hawk" was put into service to make surveys of fishing grounds, but in particular to carry out fish-culture operations; in effect, she was a floating hatchery. Millions of shad fry were distributed, and more millions of young lobsters and other species. The transfer to American waters of useful species from other parts of the world, and the introduction of Pacific species in the Atlantic Ocean and vice versa, were also parts of the fish-culture operations. Occasional transfers such as shad and striped bass from the Atlantic to California were successful, even spectacularly so. Others, like the attempted introduction of *Tapes* clams from the Pacific to New England waters, and Chinook salmon from California to the Atlantic, were failures.

For many years the belief persisted that hatching operations were of great benefit, replacing the fish caught by commercial vessels. In 1900 a federal regulation in Alaska (where the federal government had control over the regulation of the fishery, unlike its role in the states) required that each company canning salmon should maintain a hatchery in which it would produce sockeye-salmon fry, replacing at least four times (later ten times) as many young salmon as they had packed the previous season. The American effort in this field was applauded in other parts of the world. In the Berlin Fisheries Exhibition of 1881 the United States fish-culture exhibit won prizes and acclaim.

Research and Education

After the death of Baird, who had balanced fish culture with a strong scientific program of inquiry into life-histories and ecology, the Commission's work was restricted almost entirely to hatchery work. The Woods Hole Laboratory became largely a hatchery. In 1916 there were more than one hundred hatcheries and substations supported by the federal government, as well as large numbers of state hatcheries. This development occurred despite the lack of evidence that hatcheries were serving a useful function. Eventually, the conclusion was reached that it was a waste of time to release into the sea a few millions of eggs or young fish when the wild populations were producing enormously more. It seems strange that this conviction was so long delayed.

Meanwhile, other laboratories were being established whose research would be directed to marine science and the conservation of fish resources. Baird wanted to include a school of marine biology in conjunction with the Woods Hole Laboratory, but this proposal was blocked by regulations of the government. Members of the faculties of some universities on the eastern seaboard were active in marine research. In 1888 The Marine Biological Laboratory was established at Woods Hole by a group of university professors from eastern colleges. Their financial resources were small, and they were given much help and encouragement from the Fisheries Laboratory. The MBL was eventually to outgrow the older laboratory. Harvard University has had a long association with marine science. Louis Agassiz and his son Alexander Agassiz had strong connections there. The Museum of Comparative Zoology at Harvard was founded about 1860 to house the growing collections of the elder Agassiz. In 1930 Henry Bigelow, a professor at Harvard, became first director of the Woods Hole Oceanographic Institution.

Numerous university-marine-research stations have been established on the Atlantic Coast in this century. The oldest include the Chesapeake Biological Laboratory (University of Maryland) established in 1925; the Narragansett Marine Laboratory (University of Rhode Island), 1937; the Institute of Marine Science (University of Miami), 1943; the Duke University Marine Laboratory, 1937; and the Bingham Oceanographic Institute (Yale), 1930.

On the Pacific Coast, David Starr Jordan, an outstanding ichthyologist who was president of Stanford, stimulated interest at his institution in marine fisheries; the Hopkins Marine Station was founded in 1892. In 1870 the American Fisheries Society was founded by fishery conservationists to promote research and conservation of aquatic resources. C. H. Gilbert, professor of zoology at Stanford, was influential in an early emphasis on understanding the dynamics of fish populations before regulations were imposed.

The importance of the fisheries to the state of Washington caused the creation in 1919 of a College of Fisheries at the University of Washington, and of a School of Oceanography in 1951. Both these institutions, and especially the former, have trained many professionals and their influence is far-reaching. Scripps Institution of Oceanography, founded in 1903, is part of the University of California. It has been active and productive, especially in the study of the physical aspects of sea science. Other laboratories on the Pacific Coast include the Kerkhoff Marine Station (California Institute of Technology) 1930; and one of the earliest state-fisheries laboratories, that of California, founded in 1917.

Private institutions that made a significant contribution to marine research included the Carnegie Institution of Washington, D.C. In 1904 it established the Dry Tortugas Laboratory in Florida. From that time until the laboratory closed in 1939 its staff and visitors produced an impressive number of papers on the marine animals of the area and of the environment—33 volumes of reports. The Academy of Natural Sciences of Philadelphia was established in 1947, the Allen Hancock Foundation for Scientific Research in Los Angeles in 1940, and the California Academy of Sciences in San Francisco in 1853.

Compacts and Treaties

More often than not fish populations span political boundaries, requiring joint action by more than one government if rational conservation is to be practiced. Unilateral actions among states on the American seaboard produced many vexations, and failure by neighboring states to collaborate in regulations has commonly canceled any good effects these might have had. This sort of problem has not been solved, but considerable progress was made following the principle established by the formation of interstate-fishery compacts, beginning with the Atlantic States Marine Fisheries Commission in 1942. These commissions have no regulatory power, but the opportunity of their government administrators to meet and discuss mutual problems, and of their scientists to compare research results and coordinate work, has had beneficial results.

On the international level the problems have been more severe, and understanding harder to come by. With the rapid increase in high-seas fishing, interference with fleets of another country becomes more common, and dangers of depletion more likely.

The first international treaty promulgated to protect a marine resource was the Fur Seal Treaty of 1911, achieving an agreement among the United States, Russia, Canada, and Japan. By prohibiting pelagic sealing and by other measures, this treaty made it possible to restore damaged seal herds to high productive levels. It was replaced in 1944 by a new treaty involving only Canada and the United States.

The international conservation agreement resulting in the most successful example of the management of a high-seas fishery to this writing was the halibut convention creating the International Fisheries Commission in 1925. Under the leadership of William F. Thompson, a student of Gilbert, the scientific staff of the Commission succeeded in rebuilding the stocks of halibut of the North Pacific from very low levels. Thompson was also responsible for the early research of the International Pacific Salmon Fisheries Commission, whose mandate from its parent governments, Canada and the United States, was to restore the reduced runs of sockeye salmon in the Fraser River system. This body, created in 1937, has had notable success too, by eliminating blockades to spawning runs in the river, and by controlled fishing. Thompson must be credited with one of the most successful and influential careers in the history of conservation in this country.

The success of these early essays into international cooperation in fishery research and conservation encouraged the United States to seek other agreements. In 1951 this country and Costa Rica entered into a joint study of the yellowfin and skipjack tuna stocks of the Pacific, with the signing of the Inter-American Tropical Tuna Commission. This study has increased greatly our knowledge of the dynamics of tunas. In 1950 the United States was one of ten countries to create the International Commission for the Northwest Atlantic Fisheries, to study the complex mixed fisheries of the Grand Banks and adjacent areas.

Japan, Canada, and the United States were parties to an agreement signed in 1953, the International North Pacific Fisheries Commission, whose task was to study and protect the fisheries of that region. The treaty contained the concept of abstention. This concept states that if a country has been engaged traditionally in a particular fishery, if she has investigated this fishery scientifically, if she has shown the stocks to be under maximum exploitation, and if she has restricted the activities of her own fishermen to maintain these stocks, then another country should abstain from entering the fishery and thus reduce the stock below levels of maximum yield, or take part of the catch from the fishermen of the first nation. In 1964 the Japanese asked for a revision of the treaty, objecting to the concept of abstention as restricting the activities of her fishermen.

The Alaska Salmon Fishery

In 1947 W. F. Thompson, former head of the Halibut and Salmon Commissions, undertook the directorship of the Fisheries Research Institute, an organization established to conduct research on the salmon fisheries of Alaska. It was unique in being financed by the salmon-canning industry. That the fishing industry should feel constrained to finance research that seems clearly to be the responsibility of governments leads to one of the most controversial chapters of conservation history in the United States—the Alaska salmon story.

Perhaps the richest resource acquired by the United States from Russia in 1867 with the purchase of Alaska was the salmon fishery. Production reached a peak in 1936 when 750 million pounds were packed. But in January, 1960, the first elected governor of the new state told the Legislature that their state had been "handed the depleted remnants of what was once a rich and prolific fishery." This bitter statement culminated decades of complaint by the residents of Alaska over the activities and policies of the U.S. Fish Commission and its successors. The federal government was accused of failing to prevent depletion of the salmon, and of favoring absentee canning companies at the expense of local industry. A too-slow accumulation of biological information on the salmon prevented the implementation of recommendations of a succession of experts who examined the situation, including Tarlton Bean in the 1880's and D. S. Jordan of Stanford in 1904.

The prevailing view of the time that hatcheries were the answer to declining fish stocks unfortunately diverted attention of administrators from necessary research. From 1909 to 1920 the federal government spent $525,000 directly on salmon hatcheries, and an additional $600,000 in tax rebates to canning companies for operating private hatcheries. In the same period they spent $456,000 on research. When disillusionment set in, pressure increased for abolition of fish traps (an efficient, expensive type of gear owned by the canning companies), and restrictive legislation against fishing was pressed. Eventually, after bitter conflicts between the canning industry and Alaska residents a compromise law, based on a bill by Congressman Wallace White of Maine, was passed in 1924. An important regulation included in the White Act was to specify that at least 50 per cent of the salmon of a particular run were to be allowed to escape and spawn. Widely hailed as a landmark in American conservation, the White Act nonetheless had major weaknesses. No evidence existed that a salmon stock required half of its individuals to spawn in order to maintain itself. Furthermore, the Fish Commission could not measure the catch or the escapement accurately enough to enforce the regulation.

The failure of the hatcheries and of regulations like those of the White Act to check the downward trend of the salmon catches was what prompted the canning industry in the late 1940's to pay for its own research. Before long the Fisheries Research Institute was spending more money on salmon research than the federal government. Its findings were very useful to the controlling agency, but regardless of their validity the government was in the difficult position of using the industry's information to control that industry.

Law and Regulation

The pattern of fishery regulations today is similar to that described for colonial times and during the early years of the nation. The Constitution of the United States assigns responsibility for regulation and conservation of the marine-fish resources to the states (except where an international treaty is involved).

The kinds of regulations have been similar for all states, measures being largely restrictive rather than positive in nature. This is inevitable in the circumstances, since it is nearly impossible to alter the marine environment for its improvement. An attempt at positive measures was made when hatcheries were popular; but, as we have seen, these were shown to have no significant beneficial effect on the abundance of marine fishes.

Through lack of understanding of true depletion, in contrast to reduced catches that inevitably follow normal exploitation, restrictions have been imposed prematurely on a great many—probably a majority—of American fisheries. And in those fisheries where depletion really has occurred, regulations have all too commonly been of a kind that reduced efficiency instead of concentrating attention on the real problem, the reduction of fishing effort to control the total catch.

The marine-fishery laws of the United States are nearly always justified by a supposed need for "conservation," whereas their real basis, whether admitted and understood or not, is often economic. Thus the regulation favors some segment of the industry or serves a marketing or other non-conservation purpose. For example, minimum-size limits, proclaimed as necessary to perpetuate the stock, are commonly set by the minimum size the industry prefers; maximum-size limits are encouraged because very large fish cannot be sold at a profit; closed seasons often coincide with poor-fishing weather or seasons of slack markets; prohibitions of certain kinds of gear and fishing methods, justified on grounds that these are destructive, often simply reflect the dominance of one competing segment of the industry or of the public. Many of these falsely based regulations are the result of open power struggles; others are the result of sincere but mistaken concepts of conservation and of fish-population dynamics. Regulations based on economic factors may very well be useful. It is harmful and misleading, however, to justify them falsely as necessary to protect the stocks.

Slowly, as the state of conservation advances, and as communication between fishery scientists and administrators improves, regulations will become more rational and effective. Many states are examining their lawbooks to discover their justification, and some useful changes are being made.

Management Based on Science

The discipline for the management of marine resources began to develop in the nineteenth century. Fishery science has its roots in marine biology. An understanding of fish

stocks had to start with the description of the fishes, and collection and classification came first. Thus, in the last half of
the nineteenth century taxonomy and collection dominated the
scene. Men such as John Murray and Michael Sars, in Europe, and D. S. Jordan and Alexander Agassiz, in America,
were showing the way in collecting, describing, and naming
oceanic animals. Then came increased attention to life-histories, followed by studies of ecology. With rising concern
over depletion, fishery biology as a separate discipline arose in
the 1890's. This is also the time when fish hatcheries were
suggested as the solution to diminishing stocks. The English
biologist Walter Garstang espoused hatcheries, and so did
many American biologists, including Spencer Baird, as we have
seen.

In the 1920's the emphasis began to shift from the identity
and the biology of the individual fish to the characteristics
of the population. A major concern became the reaction of
the stock to predation by man. Another change was from descriptive and qualitative observations to quantitative measure-
ment of growth and mortality and of changes in population
size.

The "size criterion for catch" concept arose at this point,
in about the second and third decades of the present century.
This concept argues that for each species there is a minimum
size below which no fish should be caught—the size at first
spawning. An associated concept is the idea that no egg-
bearing female fish should be captured, and that the very
largest individuals should be protected from exploitation since
they are the most prolific spawners. All these concepts are
based on the same supposition, that in populations of marine
fishes the size of adult populations is dependent on the numbers of eggs laid by the preceding generation. An examination
of the lawbooks will reveal many thousands of minimum-size
laws, maximum-size laws, mesh regulations, closed seasons,
prohibitions against the taking of gravid females, and associated regulations based on the size criterion for catch. Unfortunately, the underlying assumption of these regulations is

false. There is no trustworthy evidence for any fish population that the number of eggs cast is the primary determinant
of the size of the subsequent generation. Instead, the sur-
vival of the eggs and young is the dominant controlling factor,
and this is fixed by environmental conditions.

Some biologists still argue that a theoretical maximum catch
exists for a particular population. A recent extension of this
theory is that proper conservation dictates that the optimum
catch should be the maximum economic return rather than the
maximum weight of fish. This economic maximum is achieved
at a lower fishing intensity than the maximum weight, but
both take place at a lower intensity than is applied in heavily
exploited fisheries. This condition exists because profits can
still be made from fishing even when unit catches have passed
the maximum, and more vessels continue to enter the fishery
long past that point. This in turn has led some theorists, including such economists as James Crutchfield, to propose a
limitation on the number of vessels allowed to enter a fishery
where overexploitation exists.

The application of the concept of limited entry of fishing
effort into a fishery poses practical difficulties, especially in
international fisheries. No fully acceptable method has been
devised for deciding how to allocate rights to fish even within
a political unit, and at the international level the problem is
baffling.

Progress and Prospects

In six or seven decades marine-fish conservation has made
certain gains. There is now nearly unanimous acceptance of
the concept of overfishing, in the sense that exploitation can
reduce the maximum sustainable yield. But this idea has been
tempered by the realization that depletion may not occur
nearly as soon as used to be believed, and that encouragement
of full use of the fish stocks is as proper and important a function of fishery science as restraint of fishing effort. The procedures, techniques, and theories of fishery science have been

improved. Sampling theories and procedures have been sharpened. Age and growth methods have been improved. Serological (studies of blood chemistry) and tagging methods (including the use of radioactive markers) have increased the precision and scope of studies of migration and races. Theoretical approaches to the dynamic behavior of fish stocks in response to exploitation, including the construction of mathematical models, have improved. Clearer understanding of the action of economic factors on the application of conservation measures promises to make regulations more realistic and effective.

In recent years there has been a rekindled interest in marine-fish culture. This is not the old, discredited kind of culture involving the release of young animals into the water in the hope of bolstering wild stocks, but true farming of marine animals, raising them to salable size. Although the idea remains little more than a gleam in the eye of some scientists, progress in knowledge of life-histories and culture techniques makes it appear feasible for certain high-priced species.

Difficult problems still face marine conservationists. We require more precise data on the relationship between fishing intensity and yield of fish stocks, on the causes of uncontrollable "natural fluctuations" and their prediction. We need to know more of the effects of reduction of a commercial species by fishing on the dynamics of the populations of associated animals, and on the general ecological set to which the exploited species belongs. The enormous complexity of fish populations and of their interrelationships with their environment has made it difficult even to define the problems.

We need more studies by animal behaviorists and by engineers to improve fishing gear. We need more attention to the economic and sociological impact of fishery regulations. Then, the maximum sustained-yield concept accepted by most fishery scientists (leaving aside for the moment the question whether it is maximum physical or maximum economic yield that is better) is difficult to apply. In the first place the data required—measures of growth and recruitment, mortality and disappearance, reaction to fishing—are costly and difficult to obtain. Then, if obtained, they are hard to translate into socially acceptable and practically applicable regulations. For fisheries exploiting more than one species, the problem becomes geometrically more complex, while still more difficulties are compounded when more than one political unit is involved.

Perhaps the greatest single circumstance complicating the conservation of marine resources is the lack of private ownership of the resources. This condition prevents the application of the care applied by an owner, and substitutes the destructive and hasty exploitation assumed to be necessary to prevent a rival from gaining the advantage.

Of the many unsolved problems associated with the conservation of marine resources, international fisheries present the most vexing. In the past decade there has been a dramatic rise in landings of marine fish, as many nations have intensified their fishing effort. Japan, for example, sends its boats to range the oceans of the world, and its landings have increased from 4.9 million metric tons in 1955 to 7.3 million metric tons in 1963. Russia sends potent fishing fleets over the world too, and its national policy is to increase enormously its yield from the sea, to help feed its nearly 250 million inhabitants.

In 1962 Peru surpassed Japan in tonnage of fish landed, to become the leading fishing nation in the world. Peru's total fish landings in 1964 were 200 times what they were in 1947 and 47 times the landings of ten years previously.

Other nations, in a less dramatic but significant fashion, are turning to the sea with greatly increased fishing pressure. Some stocks fished by U.S. fishermen are included in those pursued by other nations, even some like the salmon of the northeast Pacific and the menhaden of the coastal Atlantic, which have been regarded as exclusive national assets.

The urgency to find rational and effective ways of conserving marine fish has thus increased markedly, and mounts each day. For example, the breakdown after World War II of international-whaling agreements has put these species in extreme jeopardy. Earnest attention must be given to the problems of reasonable and effective international conservation of marine-fish resources, since without a workable understanding the newly aroused nations threaten to damage fish stocks over the world oceans to the detriment of mankind.

For Further Reading

COOLEY, RICHARD A. *Politics and Conservation.* Harper & Row, Inc. New York. 1963.

GALTSOFF, PAUL S. *The Story of the Bureau of Commercial Fisheries.* Biological Laboratory, Woods Hole, Mass. U.S. Department of the Interior, Washington, D.C. 1962.

GOODE, GEORGE BROWN. *The Fisheries and Fishery Industries of the United States.* U.S. Commission of Fish and Fisheries, Washington, D.C. 1884, 1887.

HAMLISCH, R. (ed.). *Economic Effects of Fishery Regulations.* Food and Agriculture Organization of the United States, Rome, Italy. 1962.

HERRINGTON, WILLIAM C. *Fifty Years of Progress in Solving Fishery Problems.* Gulf and Caribbean Fisheries Institute, University of Miami, Miami, Florida. 1954.

THOMPSON, WILLIAM F., and FREEMAN, L. *History of the Pacific Halibut Fishery.* International Fish Commission. 1930.

CHAPTER FIVE

SOIL CONSERVATION

H. Wayne Pritchard

When the Europeans first came to what is now America, it was a continent covered with forests and prairie grasses. The Indians lived from the products of the land, the wild game of the prairie and forest, and the fish of the streams and lakes. The pressure on the land was not great, for what is now the United States contained 1,903 million acres and about 800,000 Indians. Today this same land supports in excess of 190 million people, and the pressure on it has multiplied many times.

As the immigrants became settled, they produced crops with the agricultural methods of Europe, using some of the Indian crops—corn, potatoes, tobacco, peanuts, and tomatoes. But the bountiful and productive soil, along with the demands of frontier living, caused the farmers to be careless in the management of the land. From the beginning of American colonization erosion became a menace. This was due in part to the clearing of forest land, which exposed a shallow topsoil. After depletion of the first cleared land it was easier for settlers to move on to new areas than to maintain the productivity of that first plowed.

In the colonies, during the 150 years after settlement, tobacco became the chief cash crop, and this, combined with corn, took a heavy toll of the original soil. Colonial farmers paid little heed to the slope of the land; hence, as the slopes were cleared of trees and planted continuously to row crops, erosion followed.

U.S. Department of Agriculture photo

HUGH H. BENNETT

1881–1960

Exponent of Soil Conservation

Early Attempts for Soil Improvement

One of the first leaders to give serious consideration to soil conservation was Thomas Jefferson who managed more than 10,000 acres in Albemarle County, Virginia. Upon his return from Europe, Mr. Jefferson wrote in May, 1794, to President Washington:

> I find on a more minute examination of my lands than the short visits heretofore made to them permitted, that a ten years' abandonment of them to the ravages of overseers, has brought on them a degree of degradation far beyond what I had expected. I am not satisfied yet that much will be done this year toward rescuing my plantations from their wretched condition. Time, patience and perseverance must be the remedy.

During the years following, Mr. Jefferson adopted a program of soil conservation that was unusual for his era. He attempted to rebuild his depleted fields by a system of crop rotations, including legumes, by using fertilizers, and by several cultural practices such as deep plowing and, later, contour plowing. A leading farmer of his day, he was one of the first to adopt scientific practices, and he exchanged information with other leading farmers such as James Madison, John Taylor, and George Washington. Mr. Jefferson recognized that row crops may cause erosion and soil depletion. Convinced that soil-building programs could be valuable, he used soil-holding legumes in the rotation. He adopted a plan for diversified farming, and was a livestock farmer aware of the value of manure for fertilizer.

Thomas Jefferson was an advocate of agricultural education. In 1803 he wrote to David Williams urging the inclusion of agricultural techniques and experiments in college curricula:

> It counts among its handmaids the most respectable sciences such as Chemistry, Natural Philosophy, Mechanics, Mathematics generally, Natural History, Botany. In every College and University, a professorship of agriculture, and the class of its students, might be honored as the first.

Despite the warnings and the examples of Mr. Jefferson and other leaders who practiced and demonstrated conservation measures, few farmers adopted them. Erosion was particularly a menace on the lands of the South where cotton became the economic basis of agriculture. There was no widespread action to stop erosion. Few people recognized the damage it was doing. Land was so plentiful and so cheap that new farms could be obtained whenever the old ones "wore out" from sheet erosion, gullying, or both.

In a general way that was the pattern of the late 1700's, all through the 1800's, and through the first decade of the 1900's. During this period certain attempts were made to control erosion; for example, the "hillside ditching" or terracing programs in Georgia and South Carolina. These measures were largely ineffective because the terraces were of poor construction, because they were built on land too steep, or because they were used without the support of needed supplemental measures that would help anchor the soil.

Hugh Hammond Bennett, who is generally recognized as the "father of soil conservation" in the United States, and about whom more will be written later in this chapter, told a special subcommittee of the Committee on Agriculture, House of Representatives, October 10, 1947, about this early period:

All the individual activities taken together, however, were woefully inadequate to cope with the spreading land damage that was being caused by erosion. Farmers could see the damage . . . and they knew that yields were dropping off on many fields. They could see the gullies. They could see the abandoned fields and certainly they could see the abandoned farms that were showing up from place to place. But, as a general rule, all this was accepted by them, for some reason hard to explain, as something inevitable or a matter of course. That's the way it was on our own place in North Carolina. My father saw what was happening to his land, and he tried to do something about it; but his methods never had much of a chance to succeed on our steeper more erodible lands. The Bennetts were not exceptions, farmers simply didn't know how to go about stopping erosion. The necessary information wasn't there; it had not been acquired.

Origins of Soil Conservation

It is against this background that modern soil conservation originated. There are various meanings of the term "soil conservation." Different viewpoints are understandable for soil-conservation programs, and activities take on different meanings in various geographic areas. There are those who believe that soil conservation is a separate and distinct science, and there are those who believe that soil conservation is a combination of such arts and sciences as agronomy, forestry, soil science, biology, hydrology, economics, geology, geography, and others. Today, the term "soil conservation" has been largely replaced by "soil and water conservation."

Originally soil conservation, to most people, meant the practices that were adopted to prevent sheet and gully erosion. Today it is looked upon, generally, in a much broader way. A committee of the Soil Conservation Society of America has adopted the following definition:

> A system of using and managing land based on the capabilities of the land itself, involving the application of the best measures or practices known, and designed to result in the greatest profitable production without damage to the land.

In 1905, when Dr. Bennett was an employee of the Bureau of Soils in the U.S. Department of Agriculture, he was sent, along with W. E. McLendon, to make a soil survey of Louisa County, Virginia. As part of his instructions he was charged to determine why the locality had developed a reputation for having such poor land. He found the soil in wooded areas deep, loamy, soft, and mellow; in adjacent cutover and cultivated areas the topsoil had been stripped away leaving the surface a stiff clay that was almost as hard as rock in dry weather. Originally, he concluded, the soil in the fields had been like that in the adjoining woodlands. Tons of irreplaceable topsoil had been washed from the land a layer at a time by rainstorms.

In 1910–1911, while working on a soil survey for Fairfield County, South Carolina, Dr. Bennett concluded that about 28 per cent of the land in the county had been so damaged by erosion that it had no further practical value for cultivation. In addition he found that another 16 per cent of the area was

denuded of topsoil and less productive as a result. At a time
when the economic well-being of a community frequently depended on the natural fertility of the land, such a county was
an early "poverty" area, but no one gave it much concern.
Reports on other counties in other states showed similar conditions and indifference.

Lack of concern, Dr. Bennett stated, was due to the abundance of land in America, to man's familiarity with erosion
since the start of intensive farming, to uninformed leaders, to
inexperienced and untrained operators, to lack of surplus capital with which to adopt improved methods and equipment, to
the failure of agricultural or other scientists to recognize land
as a complex resource, and to the American custom of "waiting
until you're sick before checking with the doctor."

But Dr. Bennett himself was not complacent. Henceforth
he was like a "voice in the wilderness" attempting to awaken
agencies of government, the people, and Congress to the obvious fact that something should be done about destructive
erosion. Through his articulate ability and forthright methods
he was able to convince most of the people with whom he came
in contact about the need to take definite steps.

In 1928 the Department of Agriculture published its first
bulletin on soil conservation, entitled *Soil Erosion, a National
Menace* by H. H. Bennett and W. R. Chapline.

Late that year, Dr. Bennett presented to Congress a technical estimate of the national problem of land damage by erosion, as well as the first steps needed to start a national program
of soil-and-water conservation. In 1930 Congress provided
funds to the Department of Agriculture to conduct soil-erosion
investigations. As a result, Dr. Bennett was assigned responsibility for the studies and established 10 erosion stations on 10
important types of farmland throughout the country. Through
the information gained by 200,000 quantitative measurements
of soil-and-water losses, the public and Congress were convinced that action should be taken. As a result of the research
work, Dr. Bennett estimated that each year enough soil was
being washed out of American fields and pastures to load a train

of freight cars that would encircle the earth 18 times at the equator.

The Soil Conservation Service Established

In the meantime many states, some of which had shown an early interest in soil erosion, undertook programs of research and education in soil conservation. In 1933 Congress established the Soil Erosion Service in the Department of the Interior to apply knowledge of soil erosion and soil conservation on the farms of the country. Within 18 months 41 soil-and-water-conservation-demonstration projects were established and about 50 Civilian Conservation Corps camps were assigned to erosion-control work.

When the Soil Erosion Service was transferred to the Department of Agriculture in 1935, the Secretary ordered the consolidation of all departmental erosion-control activities. In that same year the Soil Conservation Service became a bureau of the Department of Agriculture to which was transferred the functions of the Soil Erosion Service.

By June 30, 1936, the Soil Conservation Service had in operation 147 demonstration projects averaging 25,000 to 30,000 acres each; 48 soil-conservation nurseries; 23 research stations; and 454 Civilian Conservation Corps camps. More than 50,000 farmers in the demonstration areas had applied conservation plans on some 5 million acres.

Experience indicated that local landowners should handle organization, promotion, and administrative details, so that the professional conservationist could spend his time providing technical help to the farmer. In addition, it was found that farmer promotion of the idea of soil-conservation practices led to readier acceptance. Thus, Henry A. Wallace, Secretary of Agriculture, decreed that after July 1, 1937, all erosion-control work on private lands, including new demonstration projects, be undertaken by the Soil Conservation Service only through legally constituted soil-conservation associations.

Soil-Conservation Districts Formed

Out of this ruling, and in the interest of developing a national program, President Franklin D. Roosevelt in February, 1937, submitted to the governors of all states a standard state-soil-conservation-district law, which proposed that authority be given to farmers and ranchers to organize districts solely for the conservation of soil and water. The legislatures of 22 states passed laws that year and other states soon followed. Dr. Bennett was proud that the Brown Creek Soil Conservation District in Anson County, North Carolina, his home county, was the first soil-conservation district in the nation.

By 1964, 2,950 soil-conservation districts were in existence. They had been accepted by farmers, businessmen, and agricultural agencies because of the organizational arrangement that gave them local leadership under state law while at the same time allowing the districts to sign agreements with federal and state agencies, as well as private groups, offering services to the farmers. Such services consisted of agronomic, engineering, and other technical assistance relating to erosion control and fertility development on the farm or ranch. Local soil-conservation districts, governed by a board of supervisors serving without pay, established policy and priority for services to farmers.

Other agencies also signed cooperative agreements at the state and local level. Agricultural extension services agreed to provide educational assistance to the local districts. Agricultural experiment stations agreed to carry out research needed for the program.

Other Programs Started

During the time the Soil Conservation Service was becoming established, other programs were operating to speed the application of soil-conservation practices on the land. For example, starting in 1936, under provisions of the Soil Conservation and Domestic Allotment Act the federal government made grants, later known as incentive payments, to farmers cooperating in soil-conserving and soil-building programs. During the intervening years the program of incentive payments went under various names, but is now known as the Agricultural Conservation Program administered by the Agricultural Stabilization and Conservation Service of the Department of Agriculture. Through this agency the federal government shares with the farmer the cost of applying certain soil-and-water-conservation practices; the Soil Conservation Service provides him with technical assistance in designing the practices he applies on his land.

As the soil-conservation programs became generally accepted, other agencies of government began to work in this area. The Farmers Home Administration allowed loans for conservation practices; the Agricultural Research Service, the Economic Research Service, and other agencies within the Department of Agriculture strengthened their soil-conservation programs. In the Department of the Interior, the Bureau of Indian Affairs, the Bureau of Reclamation, and the Bureau of Land Management adopted soil-conserving programs on the public lands under their jurisdiction, as did the Department of Defense at its installations.

In addition to the basic legislation, other related bills passed Congress; for example, the Omnibus Flood Control Act of 1936. This was followed by the Flood Control Act of 1944. A small watershed program was launched with the passage of the Watershed Protection and Flood Prevention Act of 1954. All agencies of government owning land have soil-conserving programs.

Two national organizations are playing important roles directly related to soil-and-water conservation in addition to other organizations in the resources field that have recognized the need to support the movement. The National Association of Soil and Water Conservation Districts was organized in 1946.

It is a voluntary, non-governmental organization representing approximately 2,950 local districts in all states, Puerto Rico, and the Virgin Islands. Its headquarters is in League City, Texas. The national executive secretary and his staff are located in Washington, D.C.

The Soil Conservation Society of America was activated in 1944 and has a membership in excess of 10,500. Founder of the Society was Hugh H. Bennett, who foresaw the need for an organization whereby technical and professional men and women employed or holding leadership positions in the new area of soil conservation might find a common meeting ground. The Society is a non-profit organization incorporated in the District of Columbia as an educational and scientific organization. It publishes the bimonthly *Journal of Soil and Water Conservation*. Its headquarters is at Ankeny, Iowa.

Conservation on the March

Today, interest in soil-and-water conservation is widespread. Farmers and ranchers have generally accepted the programs designed to increase conservation practices. As of June 30, 1964, the 2,971 soil-conservation districts had enrolled a total of 1,998,252 cooperating farmers and ranchers. By March 1, 1965, locally organized groups had made 2,247 applications under Public Law 566 for assistance in planning and carrying out conservation work on entire watersheds. Of this number, 1,065 had been approved for planning. Other programs related to soil and water conservation have made similar progress.

Surveys taken in recent years indicate that while much has been accomplished since Dr. Bennett made the soil survey in Louisa County, Virginia, there is much yet to be done. The report of the National Inventory of Soil and Water Conservation Needs, a U.S. Department of Agriculture study, completed in 1962, indicated that 62 per cent of the cropland still needs conservation practices to control erosion and maintain fertility.

The same report outlined that 73 per cent of the pasture and range land and 55 per cent of the forest and woodlands, in private ownership, are in need of conservation practices.

In summary, soil-conserving programs in the United States have been in existence for thirty years. They are firmly established and generally accepted. Moreover, soil-conserving practices are being widely used by highway departments, by developers of urban and industrial lands, and by administrators of public projects and on public land. Government and people have taken steps to protect their basic soil-and-water resources.

For Further Reading

BAKER, GLADYS L., RASMUSSEN, WAYNE D., WISER, VIVIAN, and PORTER, JANE M. *Century of Service: The First 100 Years of the United States Department of Agriculture.* U.S. Government Printing Office, Washington, D.C. 1963.

BEAR, FIRMAN E. *Earth—The Stuff of Life.* Oklahoma University Press, Norman, Okla. 1962.

BENNETT, HUGH HAMMOND. *Elements of Soil Conservation.* McGraw-Hill Book Co., Inc., New York. 1955.

COMMISSION ON CONSERVATION. *Conservation—in the People's Hands.* American Association of School Administrators, Washington, D.C. 1964.

LORD, RUSSELL. *The Care of the Earth: A History of Husbandry.* Thomas Nelson & Sons, New York. 1962.

SCARSETH, GEORGE D. *Man and His Earth.* State University Press, Ames, Iowa. 1962.

CHAPTER SIX

WATER CONSERVATION

Watershed Management

William E. Sopper

Water is undoubtedly our most important resource, since without it all life would perish. It has been often quoted as "our most important servant and one of our greatest enemies." And yet, for a resource so essential to our lives, it is almost impossible to attach to it an economic value. It has the peculiar quality of being an inexhaustible natural resource that is, nevertheless, often in short supply. The total supply of water circulating between the atmosphere and the land is probably more than adequate to meet all human needs both now and in the future, but the amount of water in usable quantities and qualities, available in a specific area at a specific time, is not inexhaustible. In earlier times people looked to the water supply before they attempted to settle in an area. Today, people too often settle in an area and then demand that water be brought to them or that excess water be kept away.

Many of the great metropolitan areas of today could not have reached their present size without the water supplied by distant hills and mountains, the watersheds from which precipitation drains into rivers and lakes. It is entirely possible that future population growth in some of these centers may be limited by the availability of water. If our ability to manage

Dartmouth College photo

GEORGE P. MARSH

1801–1882

Interpreter of Man and Nature

water falls short of our continuing need, the entire framework of civilized life is threatened.

Civilizations have disappeared as a result of failure to recognize the importance of the watershed and its vegetative cover. In the Near East the decline of Mesopotamia was attributed to silt and salt, partially as a result of lack of knowledge and concern for proper land management. The civilization of Babylon disintegrated because for centuries the operation of agriculture had been increasingly burdened by heavy loads of silt in the irrigation canals. Extensive erosion removed the fertile topsoil and resulted in a man-made desert in Syria. The hills and mountains of Palestine and Lebanon, which once supported forests of cedar, were eroded back to bedrock as a result of extensive cutting and overgrazing. Deforestation of the mountain headwaters of the Po River resulted in the silting of lagoons near Venice. More recent examples of the lack of watershed management are the torrents in the Alps in Austria, France, and Italy.

The ancient Chinese proverb "To rule the mountain is to rule the river" is as true today as it was centuries ago. Even so, vast mountain areas in China are now a total waste and rivers are choked with sediment caused by the destructive force of uncontrolled water.

Exploitation—Old Problems Renewed

When the first colonists reached the eastern shores of North America, they encountered an almost untouched wilderness. Throughout a vast land of fertile soil a network of clear streams and rivers transected its hills and valleys that were clothed in virgin forests. No problem of floods, water supply, or pollution existed.

These early settlers from western Europe looked upon the land mainly as a place on which to build their homes and factories and as a resource that could be used to produce crops of food. Timber and water were plentiful in what appeared to be inexhaustible quantities. With a forgotten history of land abuse behind them the American settlers set out to repeat every mistake man has made since he first tilled the soil. In his need to clear the land, much of the hardwood forest of eastern United States permanently disappeared.

Moving westward the pioneer cleared great areas of natural forests, converting them to pasture and cropland. He accepted corn from the Indians but failed to follow their methods of tilling the soil. Thus, in the hands of the westward-moving pioneers, corn planted in forest clearings often led eventually to soil exhaustion and erosion. In contrast some of the northern areas were settled by western Europeans skilled in farming. These people brought with them the mixed grain, clover, hog and dairy-cattle husbandry from their homeland and found it well adapted to the similar soils and climate.

Likewise, through the South went waves of settlers, clearing and burning the forests to plant corn, tobacco, and cotton. These crops provided little protection for the newly exposed soil. As a result soil was lost through erosion or impoverished through the loss of fertility. Many of the forests and woodlots left behind were cut over, grazed, and burned to the extent that a large portion of them are still in poor condition.

Continuing westward to escape the increasing pressure of civilization pioneers found a tremendous expanse of plains and mountains. Much of the rich soil of the southern Great Plains was plowed and planted to wheat. In 1890, when a severe drought hit the plains and persisted for a decade, many of the original settlers left the land and moved west. But when the drought ended, a new wave of settlers again engaged in wheat production. In 1910 there was another dry spell, and with the bare soil exposed the dust began to blow. Again the farmers deserted the land. This pattern was to be repeated again and again until the region became known as the Dust Bowl. In the process millions of acres of farms were damaged as the topsoil was blown away.

Farther west, the pioneers found the mountains of the Rockies, Sierra Nevada, and Cascades in virgin condition with well-controlled streams and vegetated slopes. However, as a result of subsequent timber cutting, excessive grazing of range land, and poor management of game populations, these virgin conditions have deteriorated, and as a direct consequence many western mountain-stream systems now exhibit the typical characteristics of unhealthy watersheds.

During the past three centuries our country has grown from a small group of settlements on the East Coast to a continent-wide civilization of tremendous wealth and resources. Along with this development, however, our water resource has taken a severe toll.

Voice in the Wilderness

While the public was slow to realize that resources even in a new continent are not inexhaustible, a few individuals with foresight raised their voices. Of particular interest is the unusual foresight of George Perkins Marsh. He watched and questioned the deterioration of his native soil under the disguise of progress. Convinced that progress would only be possible if men used wisdom in managing the natural resources, in 1864 he set down his ideas in a book, *Man and Nature*. The book stressed the vital function of forests as watersheds in relation to floods and erosion.

Forested watersheds were nature's own conservers of water and soil, and it was evident to him that the forests would save more water if science were given the task of prescribing cutting and replanting practices. He was aware that current knowledge was insufficient to answer many of the questions he raised and that answers would come only with the accumulation of new basic scientific data. Only through research could rivers be harnessed, water conserved, and forests renewed. Unfortunately, his plea for a forestry research program was ignored.

Public Aroused

Public concern for our water resources started with a series of events concerned primarily with local problems. In 1867 a commission was established by the Wisconsin State Legislature that pointed out the relationship between forest cover and streamflow. In 1868 New York State established a Commission of Fisheries to look into the destruction of forest cover, which appeared to have caused pollution of water to the detriment of fish. This was followed by the appointment of seven Commissioners of Parks in 1872 who investigated the desirability of maintaining the forests of the Adirondack Mountains for the purpose of benefiting the Hudson and other rivers and the Erie Canal.

In 1876, R. B. Hough was appointed to prepare the first comprehensive report on forestry for the Congress of the United States. The report was published in 1878, and it is significant that more than one-fourth of its contents was devoted to forest influences on climate and streamflow. It was a surprisingly good compilation of evidence supporting the beneficial effects of forest cover and conversely of the deleterious effects of its removal on climate, water, and soil.

Also in 1876, a bill was introduced in Congress "for the preservation of the forests of the national domain adjacent to the sources of the navigable waters and other streams of the United States," and to determine what should be reserved in order to prevent such rivers becoming "scant of water." The bill failed to pass, but it was the first to attempt to create national forests and was based on the conception of their value for regulation of streamflow.

One of the first recorded actions concerning municipal water supplies was the acquisition of municipal forests for the protection of watersheds authorized by the State of Massachusetts in 1882. The American Forestry Congress in 1886 adopted a resolution directing attention to the value of public lands at the sources of streams in the preservation of water supplies and urging that those lands be kept for public use "with a view to maintaining and preserving a full supply of water in all rivers and streams."

In 1891 the American Association for the Advancement of

Science sent the following resolution to the Secretary of Agriculture:

The American Association for the Advancement of Science respectfully submits for the consideration of the Secretary of Agriculture that the future of successful and more productive agriculture depends very largely upon a rational water management, meaning thereby not only the use of water for irrigation in the arid and sub-arid regions, but the rational distribution and use in the humid regions of available water supplies by means of horizontal ditches and irrigation systems, combined with proper mechanical preparation of the soil, and with drainage systems, with the object of fully utilizing the water for plant production and providing for the safe and harmless removal of the surplus.

The present policy of forest production and of allowing our waters to run to waste not only entails the loss of their beneficial influence upon plant production but permits them to injure crops, to wash the fertile mold from the soil, and even to erase and carry away the soil itself.

It is upon these considerations that the Association respectfully suggests to the honorable Secretary the desirability of utilizing the Weather Bureau, the various agricultural experiment stations, and other forces, in forming a systematic service of water statistics, and in making a careful survey of the conditions of water supplies which may serve as a basis for the application of rational principles of water management.

First Federal Action

Finally, public awareness led to a nationwide movement for soil-and-water conservation. With this movement came federal laws to help protect and develop land and water resources. The first of these was the Forest Reserve Act of March 3, 1891, which authorized the President to "reserve any part of the public land wholly or in part covered with timber or undergrowth, whether of commercial value or not, as public reservations." This was strengthened further by the Act of June 4, 1897, which provided for the protection and administration and clarified the purpose of the forest reserves. It contained the clause ". . . no public reservation shall be established except to improve and protect the forest within the reservation or for the purpose of securing favorable conditions of water flows and to furnish a continuous supply of timber."

In 1893 the U.S. Department of Agriculture published a

bulletin entitled *Forest Influences* by B. E. Fernow in which he discussed the relation of forests to water supplies. His conclusions, based upon experimental data available at the time and supported by superficial observations, are questionable in the light of today's knowledge. But he recognized the importance of headwater conditions on streamflow as indicated in his observation that "water stages in rivers and streams which move outside the mountain valleys are dependent upon such a complication of climatic, topographic, geological, and geographical conditions at the headwaters of the affluents that they withdraw themselves from a direct correlation to surface conditions above. Yet it stands to reason that the conditions at the headwaters of each affluent must ultimately be reflected in the flow of the main river. The temporary retention of large amounts of water and eventual change in subterranean drainage which the well-kept forest floor produces, the consequent lengthening in the time of flow, and especially the prevention of accumulation and carrying of soil and detritus which are deposited in the river and change its bed, would at least tend to alleviate the dangers from abnormal floods and reduce the number and height of regular floods."

Period of Controversy

The years around 1900 might be called a period of controversy concerning the effects of forests on climate and streamflow. Although much was written on the subject, few reports were based on sound scientific data. One argument, in particular, evolved concerning the effect of forests on precipitation. One side argued that forests augmented precipitation and rendered the climate more humid. The other side contended that forests can have no appreciable effect on the water content of the great masses of air whose circulation results in precipitation. With only meager data available and no adequate proof, each side exaggerated and generalized.

Reaction also came from recognized authorities. H. M. Chittenden of the U.S. Army Corps of Engineers published, in 1909, his article "Forests and Reservoirs in Their Relation to Streamflow" that tended to minimize the influence of forests. In 1910, W. L. Moore, Chief of the Weather Bureau, issued his pamphlet *A Report on the Influence of Forests on Climate and on Floods* that likewise aimed to show that forests were an insignificant factor.

The evidence for the forest was summarized by Raphael Zon, in 1912, in the final report of the National Waterways Commission. This report was later published in 1927 under the title "Forests and Water in the Light of Scientific Investigation."

More Federal Legislation

In the East the evidence of the value of forests for the protection of streamflow was considered sufficiently established, and with the forest-conservation movement gathering momentum the Act of March 1, 1911, known as the Week's Law was passed. It provided for the protection of the watersheds of navigable streams and for the appointment of a commission for the acquisition of lands for the purpose of conserving the navigability of navigable rivers. This law was the basis for the acquisition of lands for national forests in the East until the passage of the Clarke-McNary Act of 1924, which, among things, extended the federal land-purchase policy to include lands necessary for timber production within watersheds of navigable streams.

Federal participation in flood-control activities had begun earlier on a modest scale. The Mississippi River Commission was established in 1879 to offer technical assistance and to coordinate states' efforts, but was forbidden to use federal funds for any purpose except deepening or improving the river channel. Eventually navigation improvement work took the federal government into flood-control work.

The Rivers and Harbors Act of 1917 authorized money to be used along with local contributions for flood control on the Mississippi River and flood- and debris-control work in the

Sacramento-San Joaquin Rivers in California. But more importantly it specified that examinations and surveys for flood control should be comprehensive in scope and should include consideration of the development of waterpower and such other uses "as may be properly related to or coordinated with the project." This legislation provided the basic authority for the Corps of Engineers to conduct studies for flood control and related purposes. This led to the Rivers and Harbors Act of 1927 in which Congress authorized the Corps of Engineers to prepare comprehensive studies of the major river basins of the United States. Reports were prepared on 191 river-drainage basins.

In the Flood Control Act of 1928 the federal government assumed primary responsibility for flood control on the Mississippi River and the Sacramento River. Also in 1928, the Hoover Dam was approved as the first multiple-purpose project specifically authorized by Congress. Since that time the multiple-purpose consideration has been given to all similar structures built by the Bureau of Reclamation or the Corps of Engineers.

Closely associated with floodwaters are the problems of erosion and sedimentation. Serious erosion and ruin of cleared lands in the Appalachian and Piedmont regions, and the dust storms of the southern Great Plains led to the establishment in 1930 of ten erosion experiment stations. With this move came the establishment of the Soil Erosion Service (later renamed the Soil Conservation Service) in 1933 and passage of the Soil Conservation Act of 1935 in which Congress "recognized that the wastage of soil and moisture resources on farm grazing, and forest lands of the Nation, resulting from soil erosion, is a menace to the national welfare and that it is hereby declared to be the policy of Congress to provide permanently for the control and prevention of soil erosion and thereby to preserve natural resources, control floods, prevent impairment of reservoirs, protect public health and public lands and relieve unemployment."

Up to this time much of the attention had been directed

toward the major rivers and their associated problems. The importance of upstream watershed land had not yet fully been recognized. This fact was emphasized in 1935 by a joint study of headwater streams and related waters initiated by the Soil Conservation Service, Resettlement Administration, and Rural Electrification Administration. The report entitled *Little Waters, a Study of Headwater Streams and Other Little Waters, Their Use and Relations to the Land* by H. S. Person was sent to the National Resources Committee, which transmitted it to President F. D. Roosevelt. In January, 1936, the President sent the report to Congress with a favorable message.

On June 22, 1936, the Omnibus Flood Control Act was passed, which provided for the first time a national integrated flood-control policy. It not only authorized the Corps of Engineers to make investigation and surveys of flood problems in the rivers of the United States but it also authorized the Secretary of Agriculture to make investigations with respect to watersheds and to institute programs on watersheds for the purpose of runoff and waterflow retardation and soil-erosion prevention.

Along with the emphasis of flood control on the major rivers grew the concept of river-basin development. This concept is based primarily upon the idea that a system of works can be developed together to maximize the use of all the water in an entire basin. One of the earliest examples of basin development is The Miami Conservancy District in Ohio, created in 1915. Development, however, was for only the single purpose of flood control. This was followed later in 1933 by the creation of the Muskingum Watershed Conservancy District in Ohio, which is best known for its pioneering efforts in multi-use land management for integrated recreation, soil conservation, farming, forestry, and water management.

During 1933 the Tennessee Valley Authority was established, which led the way to comprehensive regional development and which has served to demonstrate on a grand scale the interrelationship between water control and development and regional social and economic well-being.

Comprehensive interagency river-basin planning began with the establishment of the Federal Inter-Agency River Basin Committee in 1943, which permitted federal agencies to co-operate more effectively in river-basin projects. Since then plans have been developed for many intra- and interstate river basins. Although the need for such action is generally recognized, the efforts have only been partially successful because of the complexity of problems usually encountered in a large major basin and the interlocking and often conflicting interests of the people and organizations involved.

Local Responsibility Increases

Full implementation of the provision of the Flood Control Act of 1936 was delayed by World War II. About 1947 the Department of Agriculture resumed its role in upstream planning and treatment with measures needed to conserve soil and water and to reduce flood and sediment. It was further aided in 1953 when Congress appropriated funds to start work on 62 pilot watershed projects to demonstrate the benefits of combining soil-and-water conservation on the land with upstream flood-prevention structures.

This work finally culminated in the Watershed Protection and Flood Prevention Act, Public Law 566, of 1954. Under this Act, the Secretary of Agriculture is authorized to give technical, cost-sharing, and credit aid to local organizations in planning and implementing works of improvement for (1) flood prevention; (2) agricultural-water management, including irrigation and drainage; and (3) non-agricultural-water management, including munipical or industrial water supply and fish and wildlife development.

It should be emphasized that with the passage of this Act the major initiative and responsibility for projects were transferred from the federal government to the people and local and state organizations. Aimed at the solution of local problems on small watersheds, it bridges the gap between individual farm treatments and programs in major river valleys.

The willingness of the local people to accept this responsibility to solve their own problems is evident in the fact that by September, 1964, over 2,000 small watershed project applications had been submitted to the U.S. Department of Agriculture, for which planning assistance has been authorized on 1,019, and operations authorized on 602. As a result of this Act there have emerged many kinds of local watershed associations and similar organizations designed to protect, rehabilitate, and develop the land and water resources of specific watersheds.

Problem and Policy Surveys

During the past fifty years numerous federal commissions and committees have investigated national water problems and policies. Even though many did not result in any specific legislation, they all served a useful purpose by providing guideposts for future action.

Of recent significance was the establishment of the Water Resources Policy Commission on January 3, 1950, by President Truman. This Commission was directed to study and make recommendations to the President with respect to federal responsibility for and participation in the development, utilization, and conservation of water resources, including related land uses and other public purposes to the extent that they are directly concerned with water resources. Recommendations for a comprehensive policy of water resources were outlined in a three-volume report, which consisted of: Volume I, *A Water Policy for the American People;* Volume II, *Ten Rivers in America's Future;* and Volume III, *Water Resources Law.*

Most of these early studies were limited in scope. The first comprehensive investigation covering all aspects of water resources activities in the United States was initiated in 1959 with the formation of the Senate Select Committee on National Water Resources. This Committee, headed by Senator Robert S. Kerr, was authorized to study the relation of water-resource activities in the United States to the national interest, and the extent and character of water-resource activities, both governmental and non-governmental, that will be required to take care of needs for water for all purposes up to 1980. The Committee report completed in 1961 included over 90 separate studies and 32 published reports and is considered to be the most comprehensive review and forecast of water-resources development in the United States ever assembled.

Old Concept—New Recognition

The concept of watershed management is not new. Remnants of irrigation canals, aqueducts, and terraces are mute evidence in the Old World of attempts by early civilization to develop their water resources. Early interest in this country was centered primarily around forest land and the effects of deforestation on streamflow. Even today forest and range lands are still of primary importance since together they comprise about two-thirds of the total land area of the United States and represent the source of more than 70 per cent of the nation's water yield.

In recent years the increasing interest in water resources has focused attention on the field of watershed management and has resulted in popular use of the term for a diversity of activities. Hence, the term has become somewhat nebulous and difficult to define. In its broadest sense the scope of watershed management includes all aspects of water resources on all types of drainage basins whether they be agricultural land, forest land, range land, urban or complex mosaics. More specifically, it might be stated that it is the effective handling of all resources of a watershed to assure maximum supplies of usable water, desirable streamflow, prevention and control of erosion, and the reduction of flood and sediment damages. It is based upon a thorough knowledge of how a watershed functions in receiving and disposing of precipitation, the factors that influence watershed behavior, the magnitude and limitations of their effects, and how these factors can be controlled or modified by man for his benefit.

It consists of several distinctly different phases that might be distinguished as the prevention phase, restoration-and-maintenance phase, and the manipulative or adaptive phase. Protection of water quality is probably the most important single objective of the preventative phase. Action under this phase might include fire prevention as well as reduction of erosion through control of road construction, logging methods, and grazing.

The restoration-and-maintenance phase is aimed at rehabilitation of the millions of acres of both public and private lands devastated in the course of our growth as a nation. This includes reforestation, timber-stand improvement, and range-land improvement, as well as agricultural-land-treatment measures that might benefit the water resource.

The objective of manipulative or adaptive watershed management is to influence or modify streamflow. It is now generally accepted and has been aptly demonstrated that the quantity, quality, and timing of streamflow can be influenced by alteration of the vegetative cover. Much work has been done in this area, but there are still many questions to be answered through research before this type of watershed management is put into widespread use.

The field of applied watershed management is still in its infancy. Management is the application of principles, methods, and techniques developed through research. Unfortunately, although a substantial body of knowledge has been obtained over the past fifty years, we still do not fully understand the complexity of processes that influence water yield from drainage basins under various conditions of vegetation, soils, geology, physiography, and climate.

Watershed research and experimentation in the United States began in 1909 when the U.S. Forest Service and the Weather Bureau cooperatively established two small experimental watersheds at Wagon Wheel Gap, Colorado, to investigate the effects of forest cover on streamflow and erosion under the conditions of the Central Rocky Mountains. From this pioneering effort there have emerged, along with the establishment of regional Forest Service experiment stations, many watershed research units. Among the first of these were the Sierra Ancha experimental watersheds in Arizona established in 1932; the Coweeta Hydrologic Laboratory in western North Carolina; and the San Dimas Hydrologic Laboratory with its world-famous lysimeters in southern California, both of which were established in 1933; and the Fraser experimental watersheds in Colorado established in 1937.

Paralleling these developments was the establishment of soil-and-water-research stations by the Soil Conservation Service (now under the Agricultural Research Service) such as the Coshocton station established in 1935 to conduct basic research on the influence of agricultural practices on erosion losses and on various elements of the hydrologic cycle.

In recent years many other agencies have initiated research programs relative to the rehabilitation, management, and improvement of watershed conditions. Among these are the Bureau of Reclamation, Geological Survey, Weather Bureau, Corps of Engineers, and many universities and state experiment stations. These and other research activities hold the promise for more intensive watershed management in the future.

Education and Research

Education and research are two most important factors in promoting water-resource conservation and management. To stimulate interest in this area a Universities Council on Hydrology was organized in 1962. This was a voluntary organization of universities established to encourage education and research in hydrology. Recognizing the interrelation of many disciplines in the development and management of water resources, in 1964 the organization was transformed into a Universities Council on Water Resources.

Of similar significance is the passage of the Water Resources Research Act, which was signed on July 17, 1964, by President

Johnson. The Act authorizes a permanent program to help establish and operate water-resource centers and to encourage water research. Specifically, it authorizes appropriations to assist in establishing and carrying on the work of a water-resource research institute at one college or university in each state and provides grants to be available to match funds made available to institutes by states or other non-federal sources to meet the necessary expenses of specific water-resource research projects that could not otherwise be undertaken. Also authorized is a smaller ten-year program of grants to aid water research by educational institutions (other than those establishing institutes under the Act), private foundations, or other institutions with private firms and individuals; and with local, state, and federal government agencies. To carry out the provisions of the Act the Secretary of the Department of the Interior has established an Office of Water Resources Research.

An International Effort

It is generally recognized that reliable water information is the basis for intelligent water management and that the global distribution of water and the global scale of the hydrologic cycle necessitate that the study of water be international in scope. Out of this need for a better understanding of water resources and the global water regimen there evolved a proposal for an International Hydrologic Decade starting in January, 1965. The scientific program for the Decade is being coordinated through the United Nations Educational, Scientific and Cultural Organization (UNESCO). Activities in the program are varied but will, among other things, include the collection of basic data, water-inventory and water-balance studies along with the establishment of experimental basins to study the hydrologic effects of deforestation, afforestation, and conversions of land use; the establishment of benchmark stations to study long-term changes and trends in hydrologic, climatic, and geomorphic conditions; the education and training of professional personnel in the field of hydrology and water resources; and international dissemination and interchange of information.

Our water-resource problems have clearly illustrated the interdependence of individuals, communities, states, and nations. The management of this resource to obtain maximum benefit for this generation, and the next generation will require the cooperation of all people.

These recent activities are certainly indicative of the ever increasing awareness of our national and worldwide water problems and the start of a concentrated effort to solve them.

For Further Reading

COLMAN, E. A. *Vegetation and Watershed Management*. The Ronald Press Co., New York. 1953.

DASMANN, RAYMOND F. *Environmental Conservation*. John Wiley & Sons, Inc., New York. 1959.

KERR, ROBERT S. *Land, Wood and Water*. Fleet Publishing Corp., New York. 1960.

KITTREDGE, JOSEPH. *Forest Influences*. McGraw-Hill Book Co., Inc., New York. 1948.

LASSEN, L., LULL, H. W., and FRANK, B. *Some Plant-Soil-Water Relations in Watershed Management*. U.S. Department of Agriculture Circular 910. 1952.

PERSON, H. S. *Little Waters*. U.S. Government Printing Office, Washington, D.C. 1936.

PRESIDENT'S WATER RESOURCES POLICY COMMISSION. *A Water Policy for the American People, General Report*. U.S. Government Printing Office, Washington, D.C. 1950.

SATTERLUND, D. R., and ESCHNER, A. R. *Forest Watershed Management in New York*. State University College of Forestry at Syracuse, N.Y. 1963.

THORNE, WYNNE. *Land and Water Use*. American Association for the Advancement of Science, Washington, D.C. 1963.

U.S. DEPARTMENT OF AGRICULTURE. *Water: 1955 Yearbook of Agriculture*. U.S. Government Printing Office, Washington, D.C. 1955.

WOLMAN, ABEL. *Water Resources*. National Academy of Sciences—National Research Council, Washington, D.C. 1963.

Water Supply and Pollution Control

Maurice K. Goddard

Water, the fount of life, is one of the basic tools with which man carves out his destiny. Indeed, his progress through history has largely been measured by the ready availability of this precious resource and by his ability to control and use it to his best advantage. Since Nature's gifts are rarely bestowed upon man without a price, water, in its wild or uncontrolled moments during storm, flood, and drought, can be one of his most formidable foes. Further, if he abuses his gift during use, it can retaliate, destroying his physical health and limiting his economic growth.

On the East Coast of what is now the United States, our forebears found the essential elements needed for the foundation of a new and good life, and for growth and expansion—a small population, a temperate climate, virgin forests and fertile land, fish and game in abundance, and an ample rainfall feeding sparkling lakes and streams.

The importance of water in the process of wresting a new life from the wilderness should not be underestimated. It furnished the early colonist with necessary food and fiber; with avenues for commerce and transportation; and with power to run his mills. His domestic and livestock needs could be met from the nearest spring or stream, or from individual or community wells.

Because people are personally affected by the domestic use of water, they usually associate the term "water supply" with the public or private supply necessary to meet their everyday needs. In its broadest sense, however, the term encompasses every use man has for water, including not only domestic use, but also use for industry, transportation, agriculture, power, disposal of wastes, recreation, and other needs. Man's use of water, for whatever purpose, almost invariably interferes with, or changes, the balance of the hydrologic (water) cycle, or alters the water, either chemically or biologically.

First thoughts concerning the need for conservation or protection of any resource generally originate with a realization that an actual shortage of, or damage to, the resource exists or is imminent. Inasmuch as the need for pollution control is an outgrowth of man's use of his water resources, the history of pollution control is a part of the history of water supply.

Enough Water for Everyone

For obvious reasons, little thought was given in colonial times to any possible need for conservation or protection of water resources. Supplies of good water appeared inexhaustible and ample for every conceivable use. Further, biological and medical science had not yet advanced to the point of recognizing or understanding the dangers of water contamination and misuse. It is, in fact, quite probable that the dangers, if recognized, would have been discounted as being of little importance on the basis of the abundant supply.

As the settlements of the new world grew into towns and later into cities, the necessity for furnishing water to these centers of population became apparent. One of the greatest incentives, in addition to the need for a dependable domestic supply, was the need for a reliable supply for fire fighting.

During a period of approximately 150 years, from 1652, when the first crude gravity system was constructed to serve Boston, Massachusetts, to 1800, it has been reported that sixteen water supply systems came into being. Most of these were of the gravity type, using wooden pipe made of bored logs to transport the water. The first use of machinery—a wooden pump—occurred at Bethlehem, Pennsylvania, in 1754, and steam engines, also constructed mostly of wood, were introduced at Philadelphia in 1800. Four years later, again in Philadelphia, cast-iron pipe made its first appearance.

Sanitation and Public Health

Insofar as sanitation was concerned, the cities of the new nation were quite typical of that day and age. Water was obtained from public and private wells and springs within the city; refuse littered the alleys and streets; and each house had its privy. The earliest sewers in America—simply open gutters —were constructed to carry off storm water and not for sanitation. As might be expected, since the common practice was to dispose of rubbish and filth by simply throwing it into the street, these sewers soon became public nuisances from the standpoint of odor and unsightliness, if for no other reason.

As early as 1657, the burgomasters of New Amsterdam issued an ordinance prescribing that the streets were to be kept clean, and all rubbish and filth were to be deposited at certain designated places. The following year, they added an ordinance requiring the removal of all privies from the streets that had their outlets level with the ground and required that they be rebuilt where they would not become a public nuisance. While public and personal cleanliness was not exactly the order of the day, when conditions in early American cities became bad enough to be considered a public nuisance, the city fathers were usually forced by the offended noses of the citizens to take some action.

Further, epidemics swept the cities periodically. Between 1790 and 1800, recurring yellow-fever epidemics hit the colonies with disastrous results. The worst affected city was Philadelphia, where the epidemics stirred up a bitter debate in medical circles. One group contended that the cause was local in origin and stemmed from the vapors arising from the contaminated streets, gutters, and marsh areas around the city. The other group contended that the disease was imported through the ports from disease-ridden areas in the West Indies and elsewhere. Dr. Benjamin Rush, leader of the first group, and a number of physicians in Philadelphia and other cities noted an increase in the number of mosquitoes during the epidemics, but attributed this increase to the fact that the same conditions favorable to the rise of noxious gases also favored the generation of the insects.

Although both sides were wrong about the transmission of yellow fever, the controversy did bring about a move to clean up the city and promoted the construction of public-water supply for the purposes of fire fighting, street flushing, and to eliminate the public wells that had become contaminated from the filth on the streets and drainage from the privies.

In the latter instance a few people had begun to suspect that there was a connection between the wells and the transmission of disease; but, as in the case of yellow-fever transmission, they simply did not understand the process involved.

The initial effort to supply water to growing urban populations was carried out by private corporations formed for that purpose in some of the other colonial cities, but the pattern followed and the results attained were much the same as in Philadelphia. During the first half of the next century, some efforts were made by the cities to protect their new sources of supply. These efforts generally took the form of prohibitive legislation or ordinances making the direct contamination of such sources unlawful. Later, both municipal and private water companies were to resort to the measure of purchasing the entire contributing watershed to protect their water-supply source. It was not until the latter half of the nineteenth century, however, that much thought was given to either the treatment of supplies or sewage.

Water, Aid to National Expansion

Because of its many uses, water was not only important to the growth of the urban areas, it was equally important to the growth of the rest of the country as well. Until the advent of the railroads, the nation's rivers and early canal systems carried the rapidly expanding population, supplemented by wave after wave of immigrants, to the West. Waterways provided the cheapest and easiest method of inland trade, commerce, and exploration. Towns and industries sprang up in profusion on the banks of the rivers and streams in order to be close to their source of supply, and to take advantage of the transportation afforded.

From the standpoint of agriculture the ample rainfall and temperate climate normal to large portions of the country permitted the nation not only to feed itself but to export its surplus crops. This agricultural wealth, coupled with the export of its other heavily exploited natural resources and the products manufactured from those resources, brought the United States to the forefront of world trade. The country's fishery and game resources were among the world's best, and the abundance of water and waterpower were contributing factors to the country's economic growth and its industrial revolution.

Settlement of the more arid western areas of the country focused attention on a series of new water-related problems. Among these were the need for land reclamation, the need for storage of large quantities of water for irrigation and other uses, the necessity of transporting water over long distances, and questions on water rights.

Water rights in the United States are usually based on either the riparian-rights doctrine or the prior-appropriation principle. The riparian doctrine, as it has developed in the humid eastern states, accords the owner of the land adjoining the stream or any body of water the right to a reasonable use thereof, substantially unmodified in quality and quantity, and subject to the rights and uses of other proprietors.

On the other hand, the prior-appropriation principle came into being to meet the needs of the water-short western states. Originally, it meant that the person who first took water from the stream and put it to beneficial use had a right to continued use, regardless of whether or not he was a riparian owner. The principle has been modified somewhat over the years by establishment of priorities of beneficial uses.

Purification and Sewage Treatment

Most experts on sanitation agree that the America era of sewage treatment began with the establishment of the Lawrence Experiment Station by the Massachusetts State Board of Health in 1886, and the Board's report, issued in 1890, is still making contributions to the knowledge of water purification and sewage treatment. The outstanding research conducted at the experiment station stimulated significant advances in the early twentieth century. Much of the station's success was due to the exceptional quality of its research staff, many of whom were graduates of the Massachusetts Institute of Technology in the allied fields of chemistry, chemical engineering, biology, and bacteriology. Some of these men were destined to become recognized leaders in the sanitary sciences, either during their long careers on the staff of the station, or after having served their apprenticeship thereon.

It must be stressed that most of the progress in the nineteenth century in water purification and sewage treatment occurred in the last few decades. For example, by 1900, only about 6 per cent of the urban population of the country was being supplied by filtered water and, while there were 950 sewered communities, 890 of these were still disposing of their sewage by simply discharging the untreated sewage into the nearest watercourse. Only two communities were furnishing any treatment prior to discharge in 1880, whereas by 1900 sixty communities were doing so. Details regarding other early-treatment methods and processes may be found in most standard textbooks on sewage treatment or sanitary engineering.

In 1880 a German, Karl Eberth, discovered the typhoid bacillus. The relationship, which had long been suspected, between polluted drinking water and typhoid fever became known some time later and provided evidence that urban and other areas could be affected from far-removed sources of contamination. In the late 1800's and early 1900's the frequent epidemics of typhoid fever that occurred in many cities and towns throughout the country stirred up public indignation, and the public began to clamor for action.

After the turn of the century, progress in providing both sewage and water-supply treatment increased in pace—science and engineering advanced rapidly, prompted by a new awareness of the fact that the nation's coastal areas, streams, and lakes were rapidly becoming health hazards due to the industrial and domestic wastes disposed therein. Individuals and groups were beginning to awaken to the adverse social and economic implications involved in the misuse and abuse of this basic resource.

Old-treatment methods were refined, and new ones were developed, as the effort to catch up and keep ahead of the problem increased. The prevailing type of water-treatment plant in use prior to 1900 was the slow sand-filtration plant, patterned after European practices. These plants, some of which are still in use today, were quite effective, but slow and expensive to operate.

During the period between 1900 and 1925, rapid sand-filtration plants were constructed throughout the United States. This type of plant, which incorporated the use of chemical coagulants to settle out solids and self-cleaning of the sand filters, proved to be much more efficient and less expensive. Further, the development of practical methods for adding chlorine to the filtered water for disinfection and eventual public acceptance of the use of chlorine in drinking water were instrumental in practically wiping out typhoid fever in the United States.

Water-Pollution Control

The public indignation and call for action, associated with the typhoid-fever epidemics, were instrumental in bringing the federal government into action for the first time. Because the states had been accorded primary rights and responsibilities for water-pollution control through the police powers vested by the Constitution, federal powers and action were limited to the pollution of interstate rivers and lakes.

Between 1910 and 1912, the U.S. Public Health Service conducted an investigation of sewage pollution of streams in the Great Lakes region in relation to the prevalence of typhoid fever and other intestinal diseases. In 1912 Congress passed the Public Health Service Reorganization Act, which expanded the research program of the agency to permit study of other problems than those associated with communicable diseases and authorized the Service to conduct pollution investigations of navigable waters. While water-pollution studies were specifically mentioned in the Act, they were to be related exclusively to the transmission of infectious diseases.

The following year, the Ohio River Investigation Station was established at Cincinnati, Ohio, and basic research in stream pollution and natural purification was undertaken. Just as the early research of the Lawrence Experiment Station had stimulated the improvement of both water- and waste-treatment methods, the research of the Cincinnati station was destined to give national impetus to the concept of river-basin pollution control.

The Ohio River Pollution Study, a stream-pollution survey of the Ohio River Basin, conducted jointly by the U.S. Army Corps of Engineers and the Public Health Service, was one of the most complete examinations of the pollution conditions of a major river basin. This study established a pattern and was one of the factors leading to the enactment of the Water Pollution Control Act of 1948, which gave the Public Health Service the responsibility for cleaning up polluted waterways in cooperation with other agencies. Subsequent amendments to this Act established grants-in-aid programs and authorized a comprehensive attack on water-pollution cooperation with state and interstate agencies. The grants-in-aid programs enabled states to build up more adequate staff and cities to construct needed treatment plants.

Many of the states, of course, had passed legislation and established pollution control and abatement programs, and were exercising this control to varying degrees. As pollution problems became pressing, more and more states established agencies and programs to deal with them. Moreover, in a number of areas where the problems were interstate in nature, interstate compact commissions were formed to seek solutions on a cooperative basis. Similar commissions were established in cooperation with Mexico and Canada, since streams and lakes also cross, or form, national boundaries.

The fact that the U.S. Public Health Service has developed working relationships with state health agencies over the entire country has helped in creating the understanding needed to meet the nationwide problems of stream pollution. Efforts to meet water- and waste-treatment problems and combat pollution had not, however, been confined solely to federal and state actions, for state and federal action is brought about through the pressure of people, both individually and acting through their organizations. These organizations are too numerous to mention and take many different forms. For example, two entirely different types of organizations are the Izaac Walton League, which has fought for years to combat stream pollution and the Water Pollution Control Federation, formerly the Federation of Sewage and Industrial Waste Association, formed in 1928 from a number of statewide and regional associations concerned with the treatment of sewage and waste water. The Federation and its *Journal*, originally *Sewage Works Journal*, are devoted to the advancement of knowledge concerning the treatment and disposal of waste water, and the construction and operation of facilities for these purposes.

The United States, then, is currently in the throes of a massive effort to clean up its streams and to furnish sufficient good water for all uses to meet the present and future demands of its exploding population—an effort made necessary, in large measure, by the misuse and abuse of this precious resource by our forefathers in the process of building the nation.

Water Supply and People

In 1790 there were nearly 4 million people in the country. By 1900 expansion of territory, influx of immigrants, and normal population growth brought the population to about 76 million. By 1960 the number had more than doubled to around 180 million. It was estimated in 1964 that there were approximately 192 million people. Census projections indicate that the country will probably have about 266 million people by 1985.

With population growing by leaps and bounds, the industry, agriculture, and essential services required to support this growth must follow right along, or the economy of the nation will stagnate. Cities are expanding outward into great complexes or supercities. There is evidence that at least fifteen such areas are forming in California, the Pacific Northwest, Texas, Florida, the Midwest, and the Northeast. The largest of these is the Atlantic area, which is stretching along the coast from Portland, Maine, to Norfolk, Virginia. In 1950, one-fourth of the population of the United States lived in this area, and one-half of the economic power of the entire world was concentrated therein.

It is not at all surprising that the nation is beginning to worry about its future water supply, for it has now become obvious that sheer abundance of raw water, in itself, will not be enough to provide for future population growth and to assure the future economic welfare. Not only quality is involved, but distribution as well. In short, water of good quality must be available at the time and place it is needed, or it will not serve its purpose. Reuse, often many times over, will be necessary.

Warning signs have been on the horizon for a long time and numerous farsighted individuals and organizations have attempted in the past to focus attention on some of our water problems. But it has only been within the past few decades that the general populace has begun to realize that water problems exist and to clamor for action.

Today's water problems are not simple, nor do they tend to have simple, uncomplicated solutions. Brought about as they are by a myriad of uses and needs, each with varying and often conflicting water requirements, they have become so intertwined that they present a complex and often confusing situation. Compounding the confused situation is the fact that water- and related land-resources functions and activities, as well as regulatory and developmental powers, are distributed among numerous different agencies, both at the federal level and in most states, and consequently, they overlap or conflict.

Because many of these agencies and most conservation organizations are generally concerned with but one facet of the whole, they have, in the past, tended to lose sight of the broad, comprehensive problem and have insisted that their particular solution or use be considered in preference to those of others. One of the best examples is the large-dam versus small-dam controversy that raged for many years between certain governmental agencies and their allied conservation factions. One group insisted that only the construction of large downstream dams could solve our flood-control and water-supply problems. The other group insisted that only small upstream dams, coupled with land and forest treatment, could do the job. While the governmental agencies involved are presently attempting to resolve their differences and have come to realize that the best solution does not lie in the exclusive use of one method or the other, but rather in the combined and coordinated use of both methods, many individuals and groups still seek to revive and prolong the controversy.

It has become obvious to most experts that single-purpose development and independent programs, designed to meet single needs and to furnish water for single uses, can no longer be relied upon to meet the multiple water needs and involved water uses of our exploding population and spreading urbanization. Further, new water uses, the increasing use of water in our everyday lives, and new pollutants or contaminants serve to complicate the problem. Many factors contribute to make our seemingly abundant supply of water totally inadequate for the future. Among these are lack of regulation, control, and good storage sites; the toll of stream pollution; the high cost of land and of relocating existing highways, utilities, homes, and businesses situated in storage sites; distribution problems; and conflicting uses.

Coordination the Key

Within the past fifteen years, a complete reversal of approach to the problem has taken place. It has been recognized that old concepts no longer apply, that complete cooperation and coordination of effort by all citizens and between all levels of government, reaching down to the grass roots, is required.

Comprehensive studies of the water and related land resources of the nation's river basins for the purpose of formulating recommended plans, encompassing all water uses and providing for the development of those resources to meet all present and future demands, are being carried out on a cooperative and coordinated basis by federal, state, and local agencies. Also involved are industries, water companies, conservation organizations, and others. As plans are completed for each river basin, efforts are being made to establish, by interstate compact or otherwise, river-basin commissions, charged with the task of implementing the comprehensive plans and with administering and developing the basin's water and related land resources. While the initial plans form a basis for beginning the task in each basin, they must be revised and adapted, over the years, by the commission to meet changing future needs and requirements.

The key to the success of this change in concept lies in the full cooperation of every citizen and in the coordination of all efforts to find a balanced pattern or plan to meet each basin's water requirements. Since the nation's serious water problems were, and are, for the most part, caused by people, it follows, therefore, that only the cooperative and coordinated efforts of the people can solve them.

History shows that many civilizations declined or fell when they reached a point in their history where a decision concerning the relationship between their water resources and their future became imperative. Some of them, of course, failed to recognize their problem or even, indeed, the fact that they had reached a point of decision. Others either failed to act, or did not take positive action in time.

The United States recently reached that point of decision when it was forced to face up to the fact that its water supply would not meet its future needs without full development and control of its surface and subsurface supplies. If pressed with vigor and imagination, it appears that the action being taken and the course being followed will assure that the nation's future economy will once again, as in the past, be based on a strong water foundation.

For Further Reading

BABBITT, HAROLD E. *Sewerage and Sewage Treatment.* John Wiley & Sons, Inc., New York. 1940.

BLAKE, NELSON M. *Water for the Cities, Syracuse.* Syracuse University Press, Syracuse, N.Y. 1956.

KLEIN, LOUIS. *Aspects of River Pollution.* Academic Press, Inc., New York. 1957.

LOOP, ANNE S. *History and Development of Sewage Treatment in New York City.* Department of Health, New York. 1964.

METCALF, L., and EDDY, H. P. *American Sewerage Practice.* McGraw-Hill Book Co., Inc., New York. 1935.

ROSEN, GEORGE. *A History of Public Health.* MD Publications, Inc., New York. 1958.

TURNEAURE, F. E., and RUSSELL, H. L. *Public Water Supplies.* John Wiley & Sons, Inc., New York. 1940.

WILLIAMS, RALPH C. *The United States Public Health Service 1798–1950.* Commissioned Officers Association of the United States Public Health Service, Bethesda, Md. 1951.

CHAPTER SEVEN

RANGE AND FORAGE RESOURCES

David G. Wilson

Man and his well-being are closely allied to the range and forage resources. With few exceptions most Americans are consumers of meat and rely on the livestock producer for their supply. In turn the livestock producer is engaged in the raising, fattening, and marketing of animals that harvest or graze plants and that convert the various constituents into products utilizable by man. With the exceptions of swine and poultry, meat supplies are dependent upon animals that convert plant products not directly consumable by man to forms that he can use. Thus, grazing animals serve an important role as "harvesting machines" of these food sources and are major protein suppliers.

Primitive man depended upon wild animals for his meat supply, but as man became more advanced he also selected certain species of animals for domestication. Because he was able to control these animals, he did not have to rely on his hunting prowess to secure meat. With improved domestication came the need for more intensive husbandry of the animals and vegetation.

What Is Forage?

Forage is that portion of the total vegetation that is utilized by the grazing animals. Forage occurs in four principal forms

JOHN MUIR

1838–1914

Preservationist of Natural Resources

—grasses, grasslike plants, forbs or weeds, and browse. These plants may be annuals that live only one season, biennials that live two years, or perennials that live for several years.

Grasses are the most important group of range plants. They usually have hollow, jointed stems, with narrow, parallel-veined leaves either basal or in two rows on the stem. Grasses may be annual or perennial.

Grasslike plants, as the term implies, look like grass but are characterized by solid, unjointed stems. Sedges usually have a triangular stem and the leaves occur in three rows, whereas the rushes have rounded stems with leaves in two rows. Both annual and perennial species are found in this category.

Forbs or weeds are annual, biennial, or perennial broad-leaved plants with aboveground portions that die back every year. Many forbs are good forage, especially for sheep and game animals, and also contribute to the excellence of pasture forage.

"Browse" is a collective term applied to perennial woody plants that are grazed by livestock or game species. These woody plants may be shrubs with several stems, or young single-stemmed trees.

Range and Forage Resources of the United States

Range is "all land producing native forage for animal consumption, and lands that are revegetated naturally or artificially to provide a forage cover that is managed like native vegetation." Range-forage resources are generally considered to be renewable and are based primarily on the sustained growth of perennial species. In certain instances, however, such as the lower elevation ranges of California and the desert ranges of the Southwest, annual forage species are the major resource. In either case management is concerned with self-seeding species. The range resources of the United States occur primarily west of the 100th meridian although in recent years range production has become increasingly important in the Southeast.

Pasture, either permanent or temporary, is "grass or other growing plants used as food by grazing animals." Pasture-forage resources may be considered an intensive form of forage production based either on dry-land capacity in more humid areas or on irrigation in the more arid portions of the country.

Permanent or improved pastures consist of perennial species or self-seeding annuals that are grown on more productive lands that are maintained indefinitely for grazing. Permanent pastures are of major importance in the central and eastern United States and are also used extensively in other regions.

Supplemental or temporary pastures supporting annual grasses and/or legumes, or aftermath of crops, are utilized to augment range or permanent pasture during periods of low productivity or when the range forage is not accessible.

The 1959 Agricultural Census listed 944 million acres of pasture and range, including cropland used only for pasture and grazed forest and woodland. The Northeast, Central, and Lake States, and Northern Plains regions had 168 million acres; the Southeast and Southern Plains regions, 264 million acres; and the remaining regions lying primarily west of the 100th meridian, including Alaska and Hawaii, 512 million acres. These vast areas are important to all citizens as they serve as the major source of our meat supply. They are also source areas for hide and wool production, wildlife, water, and recreation.

History of Resource Use

The range as we know it today was originally used by native herbivorous mammals. However, the history of man and his rise throughout the world is coupled with domestication of certain animal species. None of the New World species has been successfully domesticated.

It has been reported that Leif Ericson brought livestock to

the L'Anse au Meadow area of Newfoundland around 1000 and that Columbus brought livestock on his trip to the New World in 1493. These animals probably did not contribute to the buildup of herds nor did the horses brought to peninsular Mexico by Cortez or the cattle by Villalobas in the early sixteenth century. However, by the middle of that century, Spanish colonists were raising livestock in Mexico and Florida.

Coronado, in 1540, brought cattle, sheep, and horses to what is now the western United States. Some of these animals, no doubt, escaped and were the progenitors of the wild herds encountered by later travelers and settlers. These animals were sheep of Merino breeding and cattle of Andalusian origin.

Domestic livestock from the British Isles and northern Europe were introduced into the northeastern United States in the early seventeen century. Most of these animals were confined to settlement areas and cannot be considered as range animals. During this same period French colonists introduced livestock into the Louisiana area and into what was later to become the states of Illinois and Indiana.

The first livestock introduced into the Pacific Northwest in the late 1700's were cattle and sheep of Spanish origin from the Monterey area of California. Later British Durhams and Shorthorns were trailed in from the East. The so-called American cattle proved superior to the Spanish cattle in their adaptation to the climes of the Oregon Territory.

The Russians brought cattle of Siberian origin to Kodiak in the late 1700's, and about this same time cattle from the California region were introduced into the Hawaiian Islands. English breeds were introduced half a century or more later.

With the acquisition of vast continental land areas by cessions of state claims of the original states, the Louisiana Purchase, the purchase of Florida, the Oregon Territory, lands from Texas, the Southwest, and the Gadsden Purchase, the stage was set for the continuing migration and settlement by peoples from the East and South. Settlement, however, was not without difficulties, such as Indian uprisings, conflicts between the stock raisers and farmers, competition for forage between cattle and sheep, and sometimes disputes over the ownership of livestock.

By the middle of the nineteenth century, cattle, sheep, and horses were prevalent over most of the continental United States. Animals were trailed in from Texas, the Northwest, and the East. There followed for a period of ten to twenty years a tremendous buildup of livestock numbers and foreign investment in livestock.

In the West title or ownership of the land was much in dispute. As new states were carved out of the public domain, they were given title to certain lands within their boundaries, but the majority of the lands remained under federal control. In addition, various legislative Acts passed in the mid-nineteenth century and later provided ways by which individuals could obtain title to land by means other than purchase. Unfortunately, many of these so-called Homestead Acts were limiting as far as raising of livestock was concerned. The limited acreage was not sufficient to support a stock-raising family, although in parts of the Midwest the acreage was ample for families engaged in farming. Land grants in the form of alternate sections (640 acres) in strips 10 to 40 miles wide along railroad rights-of-way were awarded to encourage the westward push of the railroads. This alternate section plan proved to be ill-advised as the acreage was insufficient; it also discouraged sale of small parcels.

Up to this point the prime concern of the federal government was to get the land occupied. We had few obligations except to ourselves, and little or no concern was expressed over the rapidly deteriorating forage supply or the conflicts between individuals. The end of the boom period of the early livestock industry occurred in the mid-1880's as the result of excessive livestock numbers and general unfamiliarity with the regions in which livestock was being produced.

Forage supplies, previously harvested only by the native grazing mammals, were plentiful when man first introduced his domestic animals. Soon, however, this residual supply was gone and the majority of the livestock producers failed

to understand the true nature of the range. Various authors
attribute three factors as being the major contributors to the
collapse of the livestock boom. These were overproduction,
poor marketing conditions, and a combination of inadequate
rainfall and severe winters. Thousands of animals died. Many
small livestock operations were lost. And much of the foreign
capital backing was withdrawn.

The Beginning of Range Conservation

As the result of the meager trial-and-error methods practiced by the early livestock producers in the United States,
it became apparent that they were confronted with three major
problems. The first was the need for better and more efficient
animals. Studies were initiated by the Bureau of Animal Industry of the U.S. Department of Agriculture and by progressive stockmen to improve the "native" cattle and sheep by
introduction of breeds from the British Isles, Europe, and India.

The second major problem was the lack of understanding
about the vegetation of the range areas. Studies in the sciences
of taxonomy, ecology, physiology, and others were initiated
by the Divisions of Botany, Agrostology, and Forestry of the
U.S. Department of Agriculture and by personnel in state
agricultural experiment stations in the central and western
states.

The livestock producers' third major confrontation was the
realization that they were rapidly running out of new country
that could be exploited, and that measures must be taken to
protect the land resources. Some of the pioneer farmers and
stockmen of the East and Midwest practiced conservation by
virtue of the fact that they had control of their land. But,
in much of the western United States the range lands were
publicly owned, and private control was lacking. In certain
instances state livestock associations were the first to request
assistance in setting up grazing regulations.

Responsibility for the control, administration, recording,
and transfer of public lands was vested in the General Land

Office. This office was first established as a bureau of the U.S. Department of the Treasury in 1812, but was transferred in 1849 to the U.S. Department of the Interior. However, the degree of resource control exercised on the public lands was minimal.

The early 1900's mark the beginning of conservation efforts aimed specifically at range lands included in forest reserves withdrawn from the public domain by Presidential proclamation. Acts of Congress in 1905–1907 created the Forest Service, changed the term "forest reserves" to "national forests," and transferred their administration from the Department of the Interior to the Department of Agriculture.

A pioneer Arizona stockman, Albert F. Potter, is credited as being the chief architect of early Forest Service grazing policies and regulations. The more salient policy decisions arrived at after conferences with western livestock growers provided (1) that priority of range use would be established with grazing privileges allowed those already using the range; (2) that any changes in livestock numbers or herd management would be made gradually after the receipt of due notice; (3) that small operators would be given permit preference and be exempted from reduction in livestock numbers; (4) that conservation and improvement efforts would be, so far as possible, attempted without the total exclusion of livestock; (5) that fullest use of forage resources would be made consistent with good forest management; and (6) that the stockmen would have a voice in the formulation of management rules.

Grazing on national forest ranges was regulated by means of a permit or lease system whereby the livestock producer paid for the privilege of grazing a designated number of animals on an assigned range area or allotment for a specific period. It is interesting to note that at present on most western national forests the cattle range is divided into community allotments where two or more permittees graze their cattle in common on the same unit. Soon after the national forests were established, it became clear that these ranges could not be managed without close cooperation on the part of all the permittees. The Forest Service, therefore, encouraged the organization of local associations in which the members would assess themselves, in proportion to their numbers permitted, for the funds necessary to cover the cost of such items as riding, salting, and range-improvement structures. Some 800 of these associations have been in existence for more than forty years. More recently they have been the medium through which it has been possible to apply many new programs of conservation and sound management.

The public domain, administered by the Department of the Interior, was not subject to effective grazing control until 1934 when the Taylor Grazing Act was passed and the Grazing Service was established. The Grazing Service was merged with the General Land Office in 1946 to form the Bureau of Land Management.

The Taylor Grazing Act was designed "to stop injury to the public grazing lands by preventing overgrazing and soil deterioration, to provide for their orderly use, improvement, and development, to stabilize the livestock industry dependent upon the public range, and for other purposes." The remaining unreserved and unappropriated public lands, exclusive of Alaska, were closed to indiscriminate use and settlement. The lands, however, did remain open for mining claims and for public hunting, fishing, camping, and other outdoor recreation. Under provisions of the Act, grazing districts were established and grazing regulated by issuance of permits within each district. An advisory board of local stockmen in each district was authorized. Public lands not within a grazing district were also leasable. The Act also authorized classification of lands to assure proper usage and to exchange lands of equivalent value between government and state or private owners. Provisions were also made for improving, developing, and conserving the public lands.

The Wheeler-Howard Act of 1934 (the Indian Reformation Act) set up the Bureau of Indian Affairs, also in the Department of the Interior, to administer and assist on federal lands held in trust for the Indian tribes. Provisions for the conservation and development of the land resources included the establishment of grazing allotments with specified stocking and fee system.

These federal Acts and similar legislation passed by the various states have permitted livestock producers a degree of permanency on their ranches and have encouraged them to practice more intensive management of the forage resources. Another significant, although non-regulatory, conservation effort was initiated in the mid-1930's with the establishment of the Soil Conservation Service in the U.S. Department of Agriculture. This bureau provides technical assistance to farmers and ranchers on private and state lands through legal subdivisions called soil conservation districts. Technicians trained in engineering, plant, and soil sciences are made available to assist the landowner in planning his operation based on land capability classification and proven management practices.

Range Research and Education

Range research had its inception at the beginning of the twentieth century. Many of the investigations were conducted by persons trained in disciplines other than range management. Ecologists, botanists, foresters, and animal scientists formed the nucleus. The U.S. Forest Service set up the first provisions for range studies with the appointment of J. T. Jardine and Arthur W. Sampson as range technicians. Forest and range experiment stations were established at representative locations throughout the United States. Other agencies such as the Bureau of Plant Industry and Bureau of Animal Industry and various state experiment stations engaged in research activities on forage species, animal breeding, nutrition, and herd management.

In the 1930's a marked upsurge in research occurred with increased activities by the various federal and state agencies.

Where before only a relatively few individuals were working directly on range problems, research staffs were enlarged and their effectiveness greatly enhanced.

Education in range management has paralleled the development of the science. Relatively few academic degrees in range management were granted prior to 1930. As our knowledge and recognition of range problems increased, it became apparent that men educated in related fields such as forestry, agronomy, animal husbandry, and ecology did not fully meet the needs of range management. Universities and colleges, especially in the western United States, initiated programs to meet the demand for men trained specifically in range management. Since curriculum offerings at the various institutions were naturally influenced by the education of the teaching personnel and the location of the program within the college or department, a certain lack of uniformity developed.

A most significant step was the formation of the Range Management Education Council. This Council, founded in 1960 by 14 voting members representing a like number of educational institutions, has the following objectives:

To promote high standards in the teaching of range management, to advance the professional ability of range managers, to provide a medium of exchange of ideas and facts among range management schools, to provide liaison between teaching departments and organizations and agencies in affairs relating to range education and employment standards, and in other ways to foster wider understanding of the problems of range education.

In 1964 the Council had 18 voting members. According to a recently conducted survey, these institutions during the period 1960–1964 granted 643 bachelor of science degrees, 135 master of science degrees, and 38 doctoral degrees in range managment. In addition, 13 other institutions offered range degrees or range management courses sufficient to qualify for federal employment under the current minimal civil-service standards. Many additional schools offer some training in range.

Range Conservation Comes of Age

The goal of range-and-pasture management is to obtain sustained maximum livestock production consistent with the conservation of the land resources. Much progress has been made in the art of range-and-pasture management in the past three decades by the judicious applications of the sciences.

Range-producing areas very widely in the type of forage produced. By and large range-forage production is directly correlated with the climatic pattern. Some areas are of limited use because of precipitation and temperature variations while others are used throughout the year. With this control expressed by climate, there has evolved certain grazing systems, such as continuous, rotation, and deferred, that have proved beneficial to perpetuation of the plant species as well as sustained or continuing production by the harvesting animals.

Research in noxious-plant control and revegetation has shown the way for reclaiming unproductive range and pasture lands. Improved varieties and strains of forage species have been developed. Control of livestock distribution and range use has been greatly improved with proper fencing and development of stock-watering facilities. Fertilization practices have been advanced, resulting in greater production especially from pasture lands.

After a delay of thirty years, Congress has taken positive action to fulfill the land-classification provision of the Taylor Grazing Act with the passage of the Classification and Multiple Use Act of 1964, which "directs the Secretary of the Interior to develop and promulgate regulations containing criteria by which he will determine which of the public lands exclusively administered by the Bureau of Land Management shall be disposed of for certain purposes or retained and managed, at least until June 30, 1969, for certain purposes."

Criteria for classification for disposal include land (1) required for the orderly growth and development of a community; (2) chiefly valuable for residential use or development; (3) chiefly valuable for commercial or industrial use or development; (4) chiefly valuable for agricultural use exclusive of lands chiefly valuable for grazing and raising forage crops; or (5) chiefly valuable for public use or development. Criteria for classification for retention and interim management include lands of value for: (1) domestic livestock grazing; (2) fish and wildlife development and utilization; (3) industrial development; (4) mineral production; (5) occupancy; (6) outdoor recreation; (7) timber production; (8) watershed protection; (9) wilderness preservation; or (10) preservation of public values that would be lost if the land passed from federal ownership. During the interim period stipulated in the Act of 1964, public lands will continue to be managed under the principle of multiple use as defined in the Multiple Use Law of 1960.

A significant sign of maturation of the range profession can best be explained by quoting directly the objectives and membership conditions of its professional organization:

The American Society of Range Management was created in 1947 to advance the science and art of grazing land management, to promote progress in conservation and sustained use of forage, soil and water resources, to stimulate discussion and understanding of range and pasture problems, to provide a medium of exchange of ideas and facts among members and with allied scientists, and to encourage professional improvement of members. Membership: Persons shall be eligible for membership who are interested in or engaged in practicing range or pasture management or animal husbandry; administering grazing lands; or teaching, or conducting research, or engaged in extension activities in range or pasture management or related subjects.

As of May, 1964, the American Society of Range Management had 4,637 members. Members come from practically all states. In addition, memberships in Canada and Mexico are increasing as well as from range areas throughout the world.

Much remains to be accomplished! Research activities need to be continued and expanded especially in the areas of noxious plant control and economics. There is immediate need for increased extension educational programs designed to implement range and pasture management programs. Activities must continue in coordinating and stabilizing range and pasture management with other land resource uses.

For Further Reading

ENSMINGER, M. E. *The Stockman's Handbook.* Interstate Printers & Publishers, Danville, Ill. 1959.

HUGHES, H. D., HEATH, M. E., and METCALFE, D. S. *Forages.* Iowa State University Press, Ames. 1962.

HUMPHREY, ROBERT R. *Range Ecology.* The Ronald Press Co., New York. 1962.

SAMPSON, ARTHUR W. *Range Management Principles and Practices.* John Wiley & Sons, Inc., New York. 1952.

STODDART, LAURENCE A., and SMITH, ARTHUR D. *Range Management.* McGraw-Hill Book Co., Inc., New York. 1955.

CHAPTER EIGHT

PARKS AND WILDERNESS

Conrad L. Wirth

Wilderness is the basic natural resource; the mother of all. It is little understood and seldom appreciated. Yet man, like all other living things, sprang from wilderness. In fact, man basically is as much a part of wilderness as any other form of life. Only in recent years has man begun to realize that wilderness can make a significant contribution to his well-being. Yet an understanding of what wilderness is and what its values are has been a topic of discussion for generations.

One useful definition of wilderness, of many advanced, is by the late Howard C. Zahniser: "Wilderness is a natural area where nature is the host and man the guest who doesn't remain."

In a book entitled *The National Park Wilderness,* issued several years ago by the National Park Service, Chief Naturalist Howard R. Stagner defines it thus:

> Wilderness is a physical condition. Wilderness is also a state of mind. Both concepts are important—the *former* in matters of protection and management, the *latter* in evaluating the benefit of wilderness, *both* in planning for the intelligent and beneficial use of this important cultural and recreational heritage.

But wilderness is many things. Wilderness is expanse. Wilderness is a whole environment of living organisms. Wilderness is the beauty of nature, solitudes, and the music of stillness. Wilderness invites man to nature, refreshment, and wonder. Wilderness is man's first hope. Wilderness persists

146

American Society of Landscape Architects photo

FREDERICK LAW OLMSTED, SR.

1822–1903

Pioneer Park Planner

where man is free, yet only where man's actions are disciplined. Man is a part of the scene. Wilderness has no human value without him. Down through the ages, man has emerged from wilderness by destroying it. He has used its natural resources to develop his advancing concepts of a higher standard of living and a fuller life.

When settlement of what is now the United States began early in the seventeenth century, most of the people who came here did so because of their dissatisfaction with economic, social, and political conditions in their homeland. These conditions had been aggravated because most of the people were denied use of the land and its resources, much of which was in the hands of the nobility and the wealthy. Much of the land, in fact, was in royal forests, game preserves, and parks.

In America the vast wilderness presented a challenge to early settlers. It was something to be subdued, and the need for protecting any portion of it was not an early concern of the colonists. Yet the beginnings of a "park consciousness"—although not a respect for wilderness—were to be seen in acts by colonists in setting aside commons, parks, and gardens in such cities as Boston, Williamsburg, and Philadelphia. Historically, this appreciation for parks and natural beauty has had its ultimate development in our present system of great national parks and in the wilderness areas of the national forests.

Movement for Preservation

Hans Huth, in *Nature and the American,* has sketched the origins of the ideas and attitudes of Americans toward nature and the nation's seemingly limitless natural resources. Nature enthusiasts, such as Thoreau, Bertram, Crevecoeur, Audubon, and Muir, helped set the stage for the establishment of the national parks. Huth also emphasizes the contributions of writers and poets, such as Freneau, Cooper, Bryant, Irving, Wordsworth, Whitman, and Whittier. While relatively few Americans knew the work of such landscape painters as Winstanley, Durand, and Moran, the romantic expressions of these artists of the great outdoors captured the imagination of prominent persons in positions of leadership.

It was, in fact, the painter George Catlin, after a journey up the Missouri River in 1832, who first proposed that the government preserve lands ". . . in their pristine beauty and wilderness, in a magnificent park, where the world could see for ages to come . . . a beautiful and thrilling specimen . . . a nation's park, containing man and beast. . . ." In similar vein Henry David Thoreau wrote, in 1858: "Why should not we . . . have our national preserves . . . not for idle sport, or food, but for inspiration and our own true recreation?"

In the late 1800's people began to use wilderness for something other than livelihood. Outdoor recreation became increasingly a typical American diversion. As the country grew, those who could afford it began to travel, to see the great natural wonders and curiosities, such as Niagara Falls and the natural bridges and hot springs of Virginia.

Public sentiment for the preservation of wild areas and the creation of parks paved the way for government establishment of national and state parks, national and state forests, and wilderness areas. Cities were laid out with provision for parks and open space. Major Pierre L'Enfant included expanses of natural areas for park lands in his plan for Washington, the national capital, which was authorized by Congress in 1790; some 1,600 acres were set aside as Rock Creek Park in 1890.

Hot Springs, in what is now Arkansas, was closed to public entry in 1832, to reserve to the federal government the right to provide for the disposition of the springs and their use in the public interest. But the fact that the federal government failed to supervise the area adequately, and tolerated squatting by settlers and exploitation of the springs, indicated no clear intent to establish a park. Inasmuch as Hot Springs did become a national park in 1921, its early reservation was, in effect, a manifestation of Congressional interest and recognition of responsibility in setting aside a natural resource for public use and pleasure.

Other actions begun in the nineteenth century to preserve

natural areas and open space resulted in some of the nation's greatest city and state parks. In 1836 William Cullen Bryant dreamed of a city park on a tremendous scale, and with the help of Andrew Downing and Frederick Law Olmsted, the landscape architects, New York City's Central Park was finally approved in 1851. Public-spirited people campaigned for years to preserve the falls of the Niagara in New York State as a public park and to rescue the area from private exploitation. These efforts culminated in 1885 in the authorization of the New York State Reservation at Niagara.

After the decline of the fur trade in the early 1830's, the trading center and fort on Mackinac Island in Lake Michigan gradually fell into disuse, and the island was promoted as a resort. Much of the land was owned by rich Southern planters, and after the Civil War a proposal was made that the island, including a military reservation, should become a "national resort" or park. Finally, in 1895, Congress passed a law establishing Mackinac as a "national Park," but provided little money to maintain the resort area, and it ultimately passed to the state of Michigan, for a state park.

In the mid-1800's, the valley of the Yosemite in California became the focus of conservation efforts of many prominent Americans in both the East and West. Probably the first white men to see Yosemite entered the valley in the 1840's; the first tourist party arrived in 1855. As the fame of Yosemite gradually spread, its groves of Sequoia trees catapulted to national and world attention as a result of the stripping of one of the giant Sequoia trees of Calaveras Grove near Yosemite. An exhibition of the bark of the great redwood in London, in 1854, created a tremendous stir among those who would preserve nature. One of those who was especially aroused was Frederick Law Olmsted.

Through the efforts of Olmsted and others, Congress passed, and President Lincoln approved, the Yosemite Grant in 1864, setting aside the area as a great public park under state administration. California accepted its responsibilities in administering Yosemite for the benefit of all the people; but although "national" in this sense, Yosemite Park was not the first national park as such. John Muir went to California in 1868 and began a movement that was to bring Yosemite into the family of national parks in 1890, following the establishment of Yellowstone as the first national park in 1872.

The Yellowstone Story

The little-known area of the Yellowstone was explored by a party of private citizens in 1870. The Washburn-Langford-Doane Expedition, with a military escort, had no idea of opening the lands to settlement but only wished to investigate the wild rumors about the nature of the country. John Colter had passed through the area in 1807 and James Bridger visited the Yellowstone in 1830, but their accounts of the vast land of geysers, hot springs, sulfurous fumes, glass mountains, and great waterfalls were not believed.

Members of the 1870 expedition became leaders in a movement to preserve the area for the benefit of all the people. Congress debated the propriety of creating a federal reservation; that is, setting aside a large tract of land from settlement. But finally, with the expectation that no federal funds would be needed and that the park would be self-supporting, it passed an Act, approved by President Grant on March 1, 1872, establishing a vast area of 2.25 million acres as a national park, to be preserved in its natural condition as "a pleasuring ground" for the people of the United States.

The operation of visitors' facilities by concessionaires in Yellowstone National Park proved disappointing, and it was soon realized that the Act of 1872 merely initiated a process of development. A period of ineffectual administration threatened the continued existence of the park and, for that matter, of the national park idea. Opponents in Congress said the government should not be "in the show business" and engage in "raising wild animals." Railroads and some local interests lobbied to permit invasion of the park, and this clouded the broader significance of the Yellowstone Act. Although, since 1878, Congress had provided some funds to protect the park, by 1886 civilian administration had failed, and Congress refused to appropriate additional money. The Secretary of the Interior was forced to ask the Army to take over the park's protection and supervision. (It was during this period, incidentally, that Army patrols performed the duties that eventually became the work of national park rangers.) Fortunately, with the new efficiency in administration by the Army, and with increasing safety to travelers from highwaymen, a public attitude of good feeling toward Yellowstone and the park idea made it possible to add new parks.

The National Parks Enlarged

John Muir and others claimed, meanwhile, that the Yosemite Grant lands had not been preserved from exploitation as Congress had intended. Appalled by the destruction of giant sequoia trees and the devastation by sheep grazing in the area ("hoofed locusts," Muir called them) he wrote many articles and aroused much support. In 1890 Congress, motivated by the idea of conservation, reserved as a national park a 1,500-square-mile area surrounding Yosemite State Park. And in 1905, with state approval, an Act receded Yosemite Valley and the Mariposa Grove. The following year the President approved a joint resolution establishing these areas "within the circle" as part of Yosemite National Park.

Also in 1890, at the same time Congress established Yosemite National Park, other forest lands in California were set aside as Sequoia and General Grant National Parks. Mount Rainier followed as a national park in 1899, Crater Lake in 1902, Wind Cave in 1903, Mesa Verde in 1906, and Glacier in 1910. The national parks were not merely great scenic areas or locations of natural curiosities, but reserves of true wilderness in most cases—"vignettes of primitive America," they have been called. Today, virtually all the parks and many of the monuments preserve untouched areas of virgin wilderness.

As the great movement in conservation gained momentum, President Theodore Roosevelt in 1906 signed the Antiquities Act, which made it possible to set aside from the public domain, through Presidential proclamation, great scientific and historic areas as national monuments.

Birth of the National Park Service

The first two decades of the twentieth century witnessed not only tremendous park growth, but the entry of some great men into the conservation movement. Secretary of the Interior Franklin K. Lane, realizing the distinctive type of conservation represented by the national parks, sought to unify their management by appointing Stephen T. Mather as his assistant. When he assumed office in 1915, Mather administered 11 national parks, 18 national monuments, and 2 other reservations totaling 4.5 million acres. Because Congress gave Mather little money to work with, he financed, from his own pocket, publicity and educational programs designed to increase "park consciousness" throughout the nation. He secured Horace M. Albright as his assistant, and together they drafted legislation that became (when signed by President Wilson) the Act of August 25, 1916, establishing the National Park Service.

Mather, as first director of the new agency, began the work of staffing and securing the protection of civil service for the positions he established for landscape architects, architects, foresters, naturalists, historians, and engineers. The professional group he gathered became the body of a Service that one day would be justly famed for its capability and its esprit de corps. Under six directors following Mather, and with increasing public appreciation of the national parks, the process of rounding out the national park system continued. In 1964 there were 32 national parks, 77 national monuments, and 93 other areas administered by the Service, totaling 26 million acres.

State Park Development

One of the first state efforts to preserve forests was initiated in 1857 by the New York newspaper man Samuel H. Hammond, when he proposed that ". . . a circle of a hundred miles in diameter" be set aside in the Adirondack region of New York State. "It would make a forest forever," he wrote.

In 1885 the Adirondack Preserve became a fact, when the legislature set aside 750,000 acres of "wild forest land," largely for the purpose of preserving a forested watershed. Over the years, this preserve gradually has been increased until today it exceeds 2.6 million acres. Its status as an inviolable wilderness area was secured in a clause written into the state constitution of 1895.

While parks administered by the states were gradually increasing in number and area, often they were not well organized and were widely separated in concept as to what parks should be. In 1921, at the invitation of Secretary Lane and Director Mather, the state park authorities met in Des Moines, Iowa, and formed the National Conference on State Parks to foster adequate park and recreational systems in the various states and to lend assistance to their political subdivisions in park development.

In 1936 the Congress authorized the National Park Service to cooperate with the states in making a comprehensive study of public park, parkway, and recreational area programs. This resulted in the preparation jointly by federal and state agencies of the first comprehensive National Park, Parkway, and Recreation Area Plan. It was in these depression years that the states, together with all the natural resources agencies of the federal government, accelerated their work in the conservation, preservation, and restoration of sites and areas, as a result of assistance by the Civilian Conservation Corps. It took World War II to stop this great period of conservation understanding and progress.

The publication *Parks for America,* published by the National Park Service in 1964, based on a study completed in 1962, covers some 4,800 non-urban state parks and areas.

Creation of Wilderness Areas

Protection of wilderness as "wilderness" in the national forests started crystallizing in 1921 with the writings of Aldo Leopold, a forester, whose efforts resulted in 1924 in the establishment by administrative action of the Gila Wilderness Area in New Mexico, the nation's first designated "wilderness." This and other wilderness areas were to be preserved in their natural state and kept roadless.

In 1926 the Secretary of Agriculture issued a policy relating to the Superior National Forest, Minnesota. The policy declared that "Not less than one thousand square miles containing the best of lakes and waterways will be kept as wilderness recreation areas." This great tract of woods and waters was called the Boundary Waters Canoe Area.

Joining the crusade for "the freedom of wilderness" by 1930 was Robert Marshall, forester, explorer, and writer, whose imagination was captured by the wilderness in the Adirondack Preserve. Through his efforts the national policy for wilderness preservation in the national forests was developed. By the beginning of 1964 national-forest-wilderness areas totaled 14.5 million acres, which are divided into four categories: primitive, wilderness, wild, and canoe areas, with each managed under different regulations.

Another conservationist active in wilderness matters was Howard C. Zahniser, who advocated a national policy and program for wilderness preservation and who has been called the chief architect of the proposal for a national wilderness system. He wrote and spoke on the subject for many years, representing as he did the Wilderness Society, of which he was executive head. From the 1930's many conservationists and conservation groups, including the Wilderness Society, the

Sierra Club, and the National Parks Association, had worked together to launch a campaign to protect the wilderness.

Four months after Zahniser's death in 1964, Congress passed the Wilderness Act, "To establish a National Wilderness Preservation System for the permanent good of the whole people." The Act will secure for present and future generations of Americans the benefits of an "enduring resource of wilderness" in a wilderness system to be federally owned and administered so as to leave the areas unimpaired for future use and enjoyment. The Act defines wilderness as "an area where the earth and its community of life are untrammeled by man, where man himself is a visitor who does not remain."

The Wilderness Act authorized setting aside over 9 million acres of land in the national forests alone, and the review of 5.5 million acres of so-called "primitive" land for the purpose of adding to the national-forests-wilderness areas. The Act provided also that similar areas may be established in national parks and monuments, and national wildlife refuges and game ranges, with the concurrence of Congress at any time within ten years.

Pressures on the Parks

Pressures on the national parks and wilderness areas have resulted in recent decades from the increase in population and the effects of urbanization and industrialization. There have been vandalism and poaching, demands for hunting in heretofore inviolate areas, efforts to exploit mineral resources and timber, and commercial pressures on the borders of parks and through in-holdings. Improved transportation has created increasing need for roads, parking places, and public-use facilities, and has led to the actual invasion of wilderness by power boats and aircraft. Over the years these pressures have caused tremendous administrative problems and have made it difficult to acquire the few remaining natural areas and open space needed to "round out" the parks and wilderness systems.

Nevertheless, important action has been taken to overcome

these problems. The "renaissance" of park conservation, restoration, and preservation movements that began with the Civilian Conservation Corps of the 1930's continued to receive impetus in the following three decades from men who were actively associated with the CCC in its various development programs. While much good was done by the CCC, this work came to a halt with the beginning of World War II. During that war, the Korean War, and the "Cold War" that followed, the parks and facilities were not maintained at a level sufficient to take care of the unexpectedly large number of visitors seeking outdoor recreation.

Progress in Recent Years

However, starting in 1955, much ground was recovered through the National Park Service's undertaking a well-thought-out, comprehensive program called "MISSION 66," a ten-year project for the improvement, conservation, protection, and expansion of the national park system. To handle the crowds, which had more than doubled from prewar years, new techniques had to be devised. Today, perhaps 98 per cent of all park visitors stay in heavy-use areas prepared to withstand these pressures, and do not invade the wilderness. Those who seek a wilderness experience may have that opportunity, but those who do not wish to avail themselves of it are no longer pressured to spread into wilder areas but instead may enjoy the vastness and beauty by being within close proximity of it and viewing it from a distance.

The U.S. Forest Service followed suit with a similar program called "Operation Outdoors," as did many of the states with such programs as New Jersey's "Green Acres," Pennsylvania's "Project 70," and others to acquire in public ownership lands that will be required for recreation and conservation in the future.

The value of these programs fired the imagination of the nation, and in 1958 Congress authorized the Outdoor Recreation Resources Review Commission, under the chairmanship of Laurance S. Rockefeller, to study the activities and needs at every level of government with respect to outdoor recreation. Following an analysis of all activities of the various federal and state agencies in the field of conservation of natural resources for human use and enjoyment, the ORRRC in 1962 produced a report calling attention to the urgent need for providing additional parks, recreation areas, and open spaces by all levels of government and by private enterprise. It also recommended certain shifting of responsibilities and a realignment of administration and cooperation activities of the federal government in order to help carry out a well-rounded-out and much-needed coordinated national park, parkway, and recreation plan.

Congress acted promptly. Within a two-year period, not only had the new Bureau of Outdoor Recreation been set up in the Department of the Interior for planning and coordinating purposes, but Congress also passed the Land and Water Conservation Act, which provides money to be allotted to federal agencies and to the states for the acquisition of outdoor recreation areas.

In the meantime a "Parks for America" movement was started in the fall of 1960 by representatives of the American Institute of Park Executives, the National Conference on State Parks, and the National Park Service, to explore ways and means of acquiring adequate lands for the park and recreation needs of the future. "Parks for America," a crusade by park professionals, following the ORRRC report in 1962, turned its efforts into an action program in support of ORRRC recommendations.

For Further Reading

BOLIN, L. A. *The National Parks of the United States.* Alfred A. Knopf, Inc., New York. 1962.

BROCKMAN, C. FRANK. *Recreational Use of Wild Lands.* McGraw-Hill Book Co., Inc., New York. 1959.

BROWER, DAVID (ed.). *Wilderness: America's Living Heritage.* Sierra Club, San Francisco. 1961.

BUTCHER, DEVEREUX. *Exploring Our National Parks.* Houghton Mifflin
Co., Boston. 1956.

CLAWSON, MARION. *Land and Water Recreation: Opportunities, Problems and Policies.* Rand McNally, Chicago. 1963.

OUTDOOR RECREATION RESOURCES REVIEW COMMISSION. *Outdoor Recreation for America.* U.S. Government Printing Office, Washington,
D.C. 1962.

SEVERY, MERLE (ed.). *America's Wonderlands: The Scenic National
Parks and Monuments of the United States.* National Geographic
Society, Washington, D.C. 1959.

SHANKLAND, ROBERT. *Steve Mather of the National Parks.* Alfred A.
Knopf, Inc., New York. 1954.

TILDEN, FREEMAN. *State Parks.* Alfred A. Knopf, Inc., New York.
1962.

—————. *The National Parks: What They Mean to You and Me.* Alfred A. Knopf, Inc., New York. 1954.

CHAPTER NINE

SCENIC, HISTORIC, AND NATURAL SITES

Michael Nadel

Of the history of early preservation sentiment in the United States, with regard to scenic, historic, and natural sites, we have only the outlines. The development of the park and wilderness idea is better documented. Ideas and action for historic sites preceded the formal establishment of parks; the formal designation of nature reserves, in the sense of our reference, was a later development.

Historic Sites

The first evidence of preservation sentiment in the United States, according to Charles B. Hosmer, Jr., was to be found in the *Pocket Diary* of Benjamin H. Latrobe, under entry of August 3, 1796. Latrobe complains about the impending destruction of Green Spring, in James City County, Virginia. At the time it was reputed to be the oldest inhabited house in North America.

Hosmer cites other early instances. Boston newspapers in 1808 protested the proposed demolition of the Old Brick Meetinghouse. In 1813 the State of Pennsylvania met opposition when it proposed to sell the Old State House, now Independence Hall.

A private movement in 1820 created interest in historic sites, although this movement did not look to public exhibition

National Park Service photo

STEPHEN T. MATHER

1867–1930

First Director of the Park Service

of such sites. An organized preservation movement clearly recognizable as such arose in New England about 1846, in the little town of Deerfield, Massachusetts, to preserve elements of the colonial frontier that were still in evidence in the homes and other buildings of the town.

Ronald F. Lee dates the beginning of the movement to preserve historic sites and buildings for public exhibition to the acquisition of Hasbrouck House, Washington's headquarters in Newburgh, by the state of New York in 1850. This "first publicly-owned historic house museum in the country" was turned over to the village trustees for preservation and exhibition.

In general, public agencies were slow to act for the preservation of historic structures and sites, even when these were faced with demolition or deterioration. Conscience stirred private groups and associations to step in. Mount Vernon, for instance, George Washington's historic residence near Alexandria, Virginia, was acquired from his great-grandnephew by the Mount Vernon Ladies' Association of the Union by gradual purchase, with title finally obtained in 1858.

The growth of public interest in historic preservation encouraged the increase of private groups of local, state, or regional character organized for the purpose. To name a few that had their beginnings in the late nineteenth century: the Association for the Preservation of Virginia Antiquities (1889); Trustees for Public Reservations in Massachusetts (1891); American Scenic and Historic Preservation Society (1895).

Hosmer sees in the 1920's an acceleration of preservation activity. "It sprang up spontaneously all through the nation as an amateur activity, and therefore it did not possess [at the time] a national organization or leadership of the kind usually encountered in comparable movements."

In 1947 a National Council for Historic Sites and Buildings was organized. Congress chartered the National Trust for Historic Preservation in the United States in 1949. Known briefly as the National Trust, it is a quasi-public coordinating body, authorized to receive "donations of sites, buildings, and objects significant in American history and culture, to preserve and administer them for public benefit, to accept, hold, and administer gifts of money, securities or other properties of whatsoever character . . ."

Federal interest had taken shape in the Historic Sites Act of 1935. Under this Act an Advisory Board of National Park Historic Sites, Buildings and Monuments was formed. Under its authority a National Survey of Historic Sites and Buildings was established, under the Secretary of the Interior, for the listing of exceptional historic and archaeological sites, buildings, and objects that commemorate or illustrate the history of the United States. The function of the Registry of National Historic Landmarks, established in 1960, is to make cooperation effective among federal, state, and local groups and individuals for the continuation of preservation efforts being conducted by these groups, and to call attention to sites of exceptional value that need to be preserved.

Federal participation in such preservation on government-owned lands was smoothed by the Antiquities Act of 1906, which authorized the President of the United States to set aside national monuments by proclamation, including historic landmarks, historic or prehistoric structures, and other objects of historic or scientific interest. The administration of these areas was consolidated under the National Park Service in the Department of the Interior in 1933. The Department makes public an annual report, *Areas Administered by the National Park Service*, which names all the areas under their respective categories, and describes location, acreage, and date of establishment.

Scenic and Natural Sites

Charles W. Porter III, chief historian of the National Park Service, once wrote: "The origin of the National Park idea is a field of study of great complexity since it lies in the field of the history of human thought. Of all kinds of history, intellectual history is the hardest to write . . ." This could not be said more aptly of the idea of nature reserves, which for our purpose in this chapter are distinguished from parks and wilderness.

George Catlin, the nineteenth-century artist, with his rich paintings of the American landscape; the Hudson River school of painters of the mid-nineteenth century; and Emerson and Thoreau, with their love for the wild, may well have expressed the conscience of those who saw in nature a valid aspect of the social culture.

Historically, the first public reservation in the United States was Hot Springs, Arkansas, in 1832, although this may have been influenced more by its feasibility as a health resort rather than for the natural phenomenon as an attraction in itself.

In 1864 the federal government made a grant to the state of California of land that included the Mariposa Big Tree Grove, which later was absorbed in Yosemite National Park, established in 1890. The first national park, Yellowstone, was established in 1872 for recreational and scenic values; but the next "nature reservation" probably was the groves of the giant sequoia, largest and possibly oldest of living things, which became, in 1890, part of the Sequoia National Park.

Natural areas are pristine communities of balanced animal and plant populations, generally free from human interference, and allowed to follow their course of physical changes without management or hindrance. They are not primarily recreational in aim, but serve as living museums for educational purposes, or as living laboratories for science and research, or for a combination of these purposes.

In 1917 the Ecological Society of America established a Committee on the Preservation of Natural Conditions. The committee was charged with preparing an inventory of all preserved and preservable natural areas in the United States and Canada. Under the chairmanship of S. Charles Kendeigh of the University of Illinois a report was prepared for the Ecologists Union (now The Nature Conservancy) describing and evaluating areas listed by a Committee for the Study of Plant and Animal Communities from 1938 to 1946. This was described as a preliminary inventory, and was published as a special issue of *The Living Wilderness*, Vol. 15, No. 35 (Winter, 1950–1951), by The Wilderness Society; its title, "Nature Sanctuaries in the United States and Canada."

Many colleges maintain natural areas for research and teaching. Cornell University, for example, owns and administers the Cornell Plantations, consisting of areas managed for special purposes, and others that are left unmanaged. A Natural Areas Committee of the faculty has jurisdiction over a series of areas other than the Plantations, which are the source of a large volume of scientific studies.

A symposium on "College Natural Areas as Research and Training Facilities" was sponsored in 1963 by The Nature Conservancy, under the direction of Bruce Dowling. The proceedings, edited by James B. Ross, were published as Research Publication No. 1. According to this publication, nearly 100 tracts, ranging in size from 1.3 acres to 23,000 acres, are owned by colleges and universities across the country. While many are on campus, areas listed are from 4 miles to 400 miles distant from campus. It has been suggested that colleges that own nature reserves far distant from their own campus, but which are reasonably close to institutions in metropolitan areas without their own facilities, pool the use of these reservations for the benefit of the city institutions to train biologists.

Private organizations concerned primarily with helping to secure nature reservations (not including parks or wilderness), which they turn over to public or private agencies for administration, have added in great measure to the movement for preservation and have done much to arouse public support. These include The Nature Conservancy, which began in 1917 as a national committee of the Ecological Society of America, organized as an independent group in 1946, and adopted its present name in 1950; Wildlife Preserves, Inc., and Save-the-Redwoods League. In addition, there are state and regional associations as well as private foundations. The National Audubon Society has a related interest in such areas, while organizations like the Sierra Club, the National Parks Association, and The Wilderness Society play a supporting role in the context of their broader programs. Some state governments, since 1960, have established their own natural area systems, and others have similar programs under consideration.

In 1964 the Secretary of the Interior directed the establishment of a National Registry of Natural History Landmarks, complementing the Registry of National Historic Landmarks that was started in 1960. The new Registry is also under the administrative responsibility of the National Park Service. Its purpose is "to recognize and encourage the preservation and protection of select natural sites irrespective of administration or ownership—state and local agencies, conservation groups, science foundations, or private parties." Criteria for evaluating and recommending proposed sites include "natural quality and character; degree of dissimilarity to other sites; importance to education and science; reasonable invulnerability to deterioration and destruction; practicable size; availability and accessibility; and sympathetic and responsible ownership."

Possibilities for marking out and protecting natural areas exist on categories of land administered for other purposes, such as the national wildlife refuges and ranges under the Bureau of Sport Fisheries and Wildlife, the public-domain lands under the Bureau of Land Management in the Department of the Interior, in state parks and forests, on privately owned tracts, and on areas under regional authorities.

On the national forests, tracts have been reserved as natural areas by the United States Forest Service "to illustrate or typify virgin conditions of forest or range growths in each forest or range region, to be retained in a virgin or unmodified condition for the purposes of science, research, and education." These differ from the extensive areas classified as wild or wilderness, or from those classified as primitive, which are protected against roads and mechanical transportation, timber cutting, and other practices not compatible with the wilderness concept, and which serve a broader purpose than the restricted research sites. In addition, the Forest Service has designated "scenic-type areas," which are significant for scenic, historical, archaeological, geological, botanical, memorial, or natural values, but which are not restricted against development and maintenance for such use.

Professional foresters, from the viewpoint of their own profession and that of the public, have an interest in the preservation in unmodified condition of representative samples of major forest types. This interest was expressed when the Society of American Foresters, in 1947, organized a Committee on Natural Areas to list such areas, according to the Society's *Journal of Forestry* (February, 1949) "primarily for the purposes of science, research, and education. Timber cutting and grazing" were to be prohibited, "and general public use discouraged."

It is for the common good that we preserve our distinctive historic associations and conserve our untrammeled natural sites. These can add to our knowledge; but more than that, they can nourish and inspire us and add to our spiritual life. When we survey what we have done, and look to what remains, we may ask: Is it enough?

For Further Reading

HOSMER, CHARLES B., JR. *Presence of the Past; History of the Preservation Movement in the United States Before Williamsburg.* G. P. Putnam's Sons, New York. 1965.

LEE, RONALD F. *United States. Historical and Architectural Monuments.* Instituto Panamericano De Geografia E Historia, Mexico. 1951.

SARLES, FRANK B., JR., and SHEDD, CHARLES E. *Colonials and Patriots. Historic Places Commemorating Our Forebears. 1700–1783.* Vol. VI, The National Survey of Historic Sites and Buildings; U.S. Department of the Interior, National Park Service, Washington, D.C. 1964.

SHELFORD, VICTOR E. *A Naturalist's Guide to the Americas.* Williams & Wilkins, Baltimore. 1926.

CHAPTER TEN

NEXT STEPS FOR RESOURCES

Joseph L. Fisher

The ultimate reason for wanting to understand the origins of American conservation must be for the insights that can be gained regarding the future. Natural resources have always been important in the development of this country and will continue to be important for as far ahead as anyone can imagine. In no small measure in United States history is the story of how our people have used their natural resources. For example, the opening up and settlement of the West may be traced through successive policies for land acquisition, such as the Louisiana Purchase and the cession of Mexican territories, followed by land disposal through the Homestead Act and other Acts, and now emerging into a phase of deliberate land management for comprehensive development.

Over most of the period of our national history Americans have been concerned mainly with using resources. Forests have been cut down and land cleared and drained to create farms. Coal, oil, and gas, and other minerals have been mined to promote industrial expansion. Water has been developed to provide navigation, flood control, irrigation, and hydroelectric power. The principal thrust has been to tame the wilderness, provide for economic growth, and raise the level of material welfare for all Americans.

Only during the past seventy-five or so years has the idea of resource conservation found wide acceptance as being of equal importance with resource exploitation. With the flowering of American industrial development in the decades fol-

HOWARD C. ZAHNISER

1906–1964

Architect of the Wilderness System

lowing the Civil War not only did the several resource industries grow rapidly, but these trends were attended by some
less-desirable features. Among these were the destruction of
many forests and certain other resources and the establishment
of a number of monopolies in resource industries. But there
was a growing awareness that the largess of nature would not
forever support unconstrained growth without more careful
management of resources than was being applied. By the beginning of the twentieth century the outlines of modern conservation legislation and practice were visible.

For a long time leaders in resource enterprises, public and
private, have been searching for a reconciliation of two approaches: resource exploitation and resource conservation.
Many have advocated *wise use* of resources as the goal to be
sought. The problem is to figure out what this means in specific situations. What value should be attached to future benefits from resources as compared to present benefits? In dealing
with resources, how distant a horizon should be kept in view?
In what ways should the indirect or side effects of particular
resource development activities be considered? The use of
water at one place on a stream may mean polluted water at
other points unless policies are adopted and costs incurred to
prevent this happening. By what means might economic and
ecological considerations be brought together so that resource
development firms can survive and make a profit in the American economic system and at the same time protect the essential
features of the resource base on which their continued prosperity depends? What are the desirable levels of public investment and management?

Some recent developments of significance for American
resource conservation may be noted. Any next steps in conservation must take these into account.

Natural Resources as Raw Materials

Natural resources thought of as raw materials for industry
and human consumption are of less relative importance in the
American economy than they used to be, at least in statistical

terms. Between 1870 and 1965, the longest period for which reasonably good statistics are available, the ratio of natural-resource output to gross national product fell from slightly less than 50 per cent to only hardly more than 10 per cent. The relative drop in employment was even greater. But during this period of nearly one hundred years gains in efficiency of production have been sufficient to make possible large increases in both production and consumption of most raw materials. For example, the 1960 "resource labor force" was less than half the size of that of 1920; yet it produced more than half again as much. To be sure, the United States imports more oil, iron ore, bauxite, lead, zinc, and many other items than it did several decades ago; but at the same time exports of wheat, cotton, rice, and other basic agricultural products have continued high. On balance this country has been a net importer of resource products since the early 1930's. Obviously, this country has a stake in enlarging world trade and investment.

These trends do not mean that resource materials are of any less basic importance now than formerly; they still support the whole pyramid of manufacture and services that make up our high, even affluent, level of living. And when one regards resources not simply as raw materials but as the total natural environment of land, water, air, wildlife, and scenery, then he sees more clearly still the timeless and fundamental necessity for conservation and careful resource management.

The scale on which resources are developed and managed has now become quite large. Commercial agriculture more and more is in the hands of a relatively small percentage of the total number of farmers and the average size of the more productive farms has been increasing. Oil companies and metal mining companies tend to be large. Public programs have to be organized on a regional and national scale in water development, soil conservation, and other fields. Large resource enterprises for the most part are profitable and do tend to follow good conservation practices. Problems tend to be concentrated among the small owners and operators in agriculture, forestry, coal mining, fishing, and other resource industries. Here the economies of large-scale operations are not being realized.

Consolidation of smaller into larger units is difficult, and the working out of new kinds of management services for groups of small owners is slow. In the wake of these and other trends unemployment and social distress have become chronic in certain local areas, such as marginal farming, forestry, and coal-processing areas.

Influence of Government

The role of government, especially the federal government and to a lesser extent state and local governments, has increased remarkably during recent decades. At the turn of the century the federal government began its large-scale stimulation of land reclamation in the western states. National forests expanded greatly during the period of the first conservation movement through the boldness of Theodore Roosevelt and Gifford Pinchot. The multiple-purpose concept of river development was clearly enunciated.

In the depression of the 1930's soil conservation became a truly national program, the Tennessee Valley Authority was established as the first federal program for comprehensive development of a river system, rural electrification became a major concern of the national government, and numerous other resource programs had their beginning. Texas and other states launched major conservation programs for petroleum. Although many of these programs could be justified strictly in terms of the resources with which they dealt, they found their main explanation as means toward overcoming the depression, creating jobs, and raising incomes.

World War II placed heavy demands on raw materials in this country and elsewhere in the world and led to a deep concern for the future adequacy of resources. The "baby boom" of the postwar years added a new dimension to this concern. Studies undertaken under government and private auspices threw light on the issues of resources, population, and economic development, although they did not lead so directly to extensions of government policy and action.

In more recent years a growing concern for outdoor recreation resulted in the establishment in 1964 of a land and water conservation fund, which would appear to be only the beginning of federal aid in acquiring and developing land and water for recreation purposes. In the same year the federal government began a program of grants for research on water resources development that promises to be a continuing program, much as federal aid to agricultural research has continued over many years.

With these spurts and shifts of focus the history of conservation in this century certainly reveals an increasing role for government. Because of the wide scale of resource problems and the need for taking more thoroughly into account the social benefits and costs of resource programs, it appears likely that government responsibility for conservation will be enlarged in the future.

Science and Technology

Another significant development is the capacity of modern science and technology not only to discover new sources of raw materials but to create new raw materials altogether. Apparently, when the scientific, technological, and industrial base of a country becomes broad enough, problems of providing enough quantity of raw materials become less difficult. Oil provides a good example of this. More efficient methods of exploration and discovery have held in check what would otherwise be a tendency for the cost of new discoveries to rise more rapidly. In addition, new means for secondary and even tertiary recovery of oil from old fields have furnished a large additional source of supply. Beyond this are the immense potentials for extracting liquid products from the hard oil shales in Colorado, Utah, and Wyoming. The reserves here far exceed known reserves of underground liquid petroleum, and costs of extraction of the liquid product from shale apparently are only slightly higher than from conventional sources. The immense reserves of oil in the tar sands of the prairie provinces of Canada offer another extremely large source that is nearing the stage of commercial production. Only slightly less eco-

nomic than these two sources is the extraction of liquid hydro-
carbons from coal, of which this country has enormous reserves.

Many problems would attend the large-scale development
of these new sources of supply. In the case of oil shale, for
example, these include: improving the technology of retorting
or underground extraction of oil, dealing with problems of
water and air pollution and disfigurement of the natural landscape, planning for increased population of the communities
in the oil-shale area, as well as settling the more immediate
problems of how to arrange additional research leading to leases
of public oil-shale land. But the main point is clear: new technology has rather completely altered the traditional view that
this country was about to run out of oil. Additional and much
cheaper supplies of oil could also be imported from the Middle
East, Venezuela, and North Africa.

But the possibilities for substitution that are opened up by
technology go even farther afield. Automobiles operating on
batteries or fuel cells could eliminate the need for gasoline.
In this instance the "fuel" might be nuclear power to charge the
batteries, or hydrogen for the fuel cells.

Efficiency in Water Use

The story of technology and substitutions is equally fascinat-
ing for water. In addition to building more dams and reservoirs for water storage are the following possibilities: the
inexpensive lining of irrigation canals to reduce loss from seep-
age, the spreading of monomolecular films over reservoirs to
check evaporation losses, the elimination of useless water-using
trees and plants in arid areas, the recycling of water in industrial processes, improved methods for treating polluted
water, and many others. The systematic analysis of alternative
sources of water supply as these are related to the variety of
uses offers great promise for the development and management
of whole river systems to yield optimum results. Another kind
of change, this one institutional rather than technological, offers
a way of providing water for the support of a much larger

population in most of the arid West. This would be by legal and contractual changes in the western states to shift water use away from irrigation agriculture toward use for domestic and industrial purposes. In the West some 95 per cent of water use is for irrigation, much of it producing crops already in surplus. It takes about the same amount of water to supply irrigation to an acre in crops as for an acre developed in small, single-family homes.

Beyond these lie the uncertain possibilities of obtaining additional water at times of need through cloud seeding to induce rainfall. Scientific work to understand the physics and chemistry of artificial rainmaking is proceeding. Another potential source of fresh water lies in the desalinization of ocean and brackish water. Methods are being tested involving ion exchange and distillation, whether by burning fuel or making use of the energy of the sun. Recent technological developments have brought the cost of producing fresh water, by various means, down considerably, but in most places the levels are still well above the cost of water from conventional sources. Long-distance transport of water, including diversions through mountain ranges from one river system to another, offers an additional way of bringing water from surplus to deficit areas.

Rising Demand for Recreation

Other more recent developments with major effects on resources might be noted. Continued increase in population, income, and mobility has combined with increasing leisure and a desire to escape from the factory and office to produce rapid rise in the demand for outdoor recreation. This includes hunting, fishing, water sports, camping and picnicking, and all the rest. National and state parks and forests, and other outdoor recreation areas are being used in ever increasing intensity; the rate of growth in user days for most of these areas has been around 10 per cent annually for many years.

The increase in number of areas and in acreage has been much slower. More land will have to be acquired for public recreation; existing land will have to be developed more intensively for such purposes; recreational use will have to be added to forest, grazing, and other land uses wherever possible; and all levels of government will have to plan on a much wider and more deliberate scale if demands for outdoor recreation that are implicit in economic and social trends are to be satisfied. Scenic resources along highways and in both rural and urban areas undoubtedly will come in for greater attention as population grows and awareness of the importance of natural beauty spreads among the people.

If the traditional interest of millions of Americans in hunting and fishing is to continue for future generations, it will be necessary to subject wildlife and fish to increasingly intensive management, which will have to be reconciled with other needs. Compromises will have to be found; for example, between draining potholes and marshes for agriculture and retaining them as breeding ground for waterfowl.

The Outlook for Resources

What then lies ahead for this country? By the year 2000 the population of the United States may be around 330 million, up by 130 million or so, and the gross national product may increase four times to about $2.2 billion. Per-capita consumption would double approximately.

To match this overall growth, requirements for fresh water actually depleted could well nearly double by 2000, timber nearly triple, oil about triple, iron ore increase by two and one-half times, the same for copper, and aluminum perhaps six or seven times. Nuclear power by 2000 might be providing 15 per cent of total energy consumption and half of electric-power consumption. Increases in agricultural requirements generally would be less, and probably that for crop and grazing land would rise only slightly because of continued rapid increases in yields. These esitmates of future resource requirements point clearly to the importance of conservation and sound development of all resources, if our country is to grow and prosper.

Will the country's resource base, its science and technology, its labor and managerial skills, and its capacity to import needed materials be adequate for meeting these requirements? In purely quantitative terms the outlook is favorable for at least several decades ahead. This opinion is supported by the long growth trends of the past and the resource supply prospects of the future. The needs of a growing population and an expanding economy most likely can be met from the nation's existing land, water, and minerals base, although it probably will be necessary to import fairly large amounts of a few materials, principally metals. Our skills in research and development and in resource management appear to be sufficient to assure enough raw materials to meet our needs without great strain for many years to come. Per-capita production and consumption of most all materials have been increasing from the earliest days of settlement, and this trend shows no sign of being reversed. Our agriculture continues to be so productive as to yield surpluses of major basic crops. Our coal reserves are ample for a long time to come, and large new sources of energy are clearly on the horizon. Substitute building materials can ease any incipient tendency toward shortage of lumber; plastic materials can now be developed to meet particular needs. We are only beginning to tap the possibilities for systematic management of our water supplies.

Undoubtedly there will be difficulties in connection with certain raw materials in certain places and in certain times, but in general the outlook is favorable in this country. In some other parts of the world where human population is dense, the resource base poor, and levels of living low, the outlook is far less favorable. Much of Asia, Africa, and Latin America will find difficulty in keeping ahead of rapid population growth, especially in food crops. And, it should be noted, this look ahead extends only to the end of this century. Beyond that a continuation of present growth trends could lead to trouble if ways are not found to alter some of them.

Problems of resource or environmental quality loom as the major ones for this country in the years ahead. Water pollution, air pollution, land pollution through the careless use of pesticides, and degradation of landscape generally seem to be increasing in severity and will call for strenuous action on many fronts if trends are to be decisively turned. Information and education about these problems can be the basis for expanded and improved policies and actions. Undoubtedly government will play an increasing role in dealing with these problems since many of the adverse effects of water pollution, for example, are borne, not by those who cause the pollution, but by others living downstream. The necessity for cooperative approaches involving both government, private organizations, and individuals more and more is coming to be recognized as essential, thereby displacing some of the public-private animosities that have been so noticeable in the resources field in the past.

It appears inevitable that both broad policies and specific programs for resource conservation and development will have to be planned in a deliberate and comprehensive way as population increases and presses harder on the natural environment. River systems in the East as well as in the West will most likely be planned and developed in a comprehensive way for water quality, water supply, and for the related benefits in recreation and other fields. One can look also for extensions of public policy in forestry, fish, wildlife, and outdoor recreation. To a limited extent public policy will probably find direct expression in land and water acquisition and direct management, but principally public policy will continue to be indirect, taking the form of specific encouragements and penalties. Education and extension across a broad front of resource activities most likely will be expanded as the preferred way of helping people solve their own problems. More and more this country will find itself cooperating with other countries in the meeting of resource problems by means of treaties, investment and development programs, trade, and shared research activities. One hopes that lessons of international cooperation learned in the more tangible and visible resource fields can be transferred to international relations generally.

Finally, one would expect the years ahead to see an acceleration of research, experimentation, and supporting education in all of the resource fields—in basic science, engineering, economics, social science, management, and policy itself. Research and education are the two best means of finding ways to prevent resource deterioration and meet increasing resource needs. In the end these, and the human beings that make them possible, are our most precious resources.

For Further Reading

BARNETT, HAROLD J., and MORSE, CHANDLER. *Scarcity and Growth.* The Johns Hopkins Press, Baltimore. 1963.

BROWN, HARRISON. *The Challenge of Man's Future.* The Viking Press, New York. 1954.

CLAWSON, MARION, HELD, R. BURNELL, and STODDARD, CHARLES H. *Land For the Future.* The Johns Hopkins Press, Baltimore. 1960.

JARRETT, HENRY (ed.). *Perspectives on Conservation.* The Johns Hopkins Press, Baltimore. 1958.

LANDSBERG, HANS H. *Natural Resources for U.S. Growth.* The Johns Hopkins Press, Baltimore. 1964.

LANDSBERG, HANS H., FISCHMAN, LEONARD L., and FISHER, JOSEPH L. *Resources in America's Future.* The Johns Hopkins Press, Baltimore. 1963.

Natural Resources, A Summary Report, Committee on Natural Resources, plus supporting studies on Renewable Resources, Water Resources, Mineral Resources, Energy Resources, Marine Resources, Environmental Resources, and Social and Economic Aspects of Natural Resources. National Academy of Sciences-National Research Council, Washington, D.C. 1962.

Natural Resources: Energy, Water and River Basin Development, Natural Resources: Minerals and Mining, Mapping and Geodetic Control, Agriculture. Volumes I, II, and III of U.S. papers prepared for the U.N. Conference on the Application of Science and Technology for the Benefit of the Less Developed Areas, U.S. Government Printing Office, Washington, D.C. 1963.

OUTDOOR RECREATION RESOURCES REVIEW COMMISSION. *Outdoor Recreation for America, A Report to the President and to the Congress.* U.S. Government Printing Office, Washington, D.C. 1962. See also the 27 supporting studies for treatment of special topics.

PIEL, GERARD (ed.). *Technology in Economic Development.* Alfred A. Knopf, Inc., New York. 1964.

THE EDITORS AND CONTRIBUTORS

HENRY CLEPPER is a graduate of the old Pennsylvania State Forest Academy at Mont Alto. Following fifteen years with the Pennsylvania Department of Forests and Waters, he served briefly in the U.S. Forest Service. Since 1937 he has been executive secretary of the Society of American Foresters, Washington, D.C., and managing editor of the *Journal of Forestry*. He is a former chairman of the Natural Resources Council of America.

JOSEPH L. FISHER is an economist with a Ph.D. degree from Harvard University. He served as a technical planner for the National Resources Planning Board during 1939–1943, then as an economist with the Department of State. During 1947–1953 he was economist and executive officer of the Council of Economic Advisers. In 1953 he joined the staff of Resources for the Future, Inc., Washington, D.C., and has been president since 1959.

MAURICE K. GODDARD is a forester who joined the faculty of the School of Forestry, The Pennsylvania State University, in 1946, and became director of the School in 1952. In 1955 he was appointed Secretary of the Pennsylvania Department of Forests and Waters, in which office he is now serving his third term. He is a member of the Water Pollution Control Advisory Board, U.S. Department of Health, Education and Welfare.

EDWARD H. GRAHAM was educated in botany and plant ecology at the University of Pittsburgh. In 1937 he left Pittsburgh, where he was assistant curator of botany at the Carnegie Museum, to become a biologist with the U.S. Soil Conservation Service, from which he retired in 1964 as assistant administrator for international programs. The author of numerous technical papers and several books, among them *Natural Principles of Land Use*, Dr. Graham is now a private consulting ecologist. He is also engaged in international ecological activities, especially through the work of the International Union for the Conservation of Nature and Natural Resources and the International Biological Program.

CLARENCE P. IDYLL, a graduate of the University of British Columbia, took his Ph.D. at the College of Fisheries at the University of Washington. He worked eight years as a biologist for the International Pacific Salmon Fisheries Commission. In 1948 he went to the University of Miami where he now is professor of marine biology and chairman of the Division of Fishery Science at the Institute of Marine Science. He is chairman of the Gulf and Caribbean Fisheries Institute. He is the author of a book for the layman entitled *Abyss—The Deep Sea and the Creatures That Live in It*.

ARTHUR B. MEYER, editor of the *Journal of Forestry*, received his B.S. degree in forestry from Michigan State University in 1938 and joined the Forestry Section of the Missouri Conservation Commission. Following service as a Navy photographic interpreter, from 1942 to 1945, he became assistant to the state forester, resigning in 1947 to enter private business. He returned to the Commission in 1949 as assistant state forester in charge of forest management; and was then named editor of publications for the Society of American Foresters in 1952. He is the author of popular articles on forestry, conservation, and other publications, including coeditorship of the *Forestry Handbook*, editor and coauthor of *American Forestry: Six Decades of Growth*, editor of *Forestry Education in America*, and coauthor of *The World of the Forest*.

MICHAEL NADEL, following more than a decade of conservation activity in New York State, during which he served as vice-president of the New York State Conservation Council, and for four years as a member of the advisory committee on fish and game to the New York State Conservation Commissioner, joined the staff of The Wilderness Society in 1955. He is assistant executive director of The Wilderness Society, and editor of *The Living Wilderness.*

DANIEL A. POOLE, secretary of the Wildlife Management Institute and editor of the Institute's biweekly *Outdoor News Bulletin,* holds the B.S. and M.S. degrees in wildlife management from Montana State University. He has worked with the Montana Fish and Game Department and with the U.S. Fish and Wildlife Service in California and Utah. A member of the Institute's staff since 1952, he also is the editor of the *Executive News Service* of the Natural Resources Council of America and writes a column for *The American Rifleman,* the monthly magazine of the National Rifle Association of America.

H. WAYNE PRITCHARD, born on a farm near Estevan, Saskatchewan, Canada, became a citizen of the United States in 1929. Graduated from Iowa State University in 1939, he taught vocational agriculture from 1939–1949 except for twenty-six months in the U.S. Army Air Force during World War II. He became executive secretary of the Soil Conservation Society of America in 1952.

WILLIAM E. SOPPER is on the faculty of the School of Forestry, The Pennsylvania State University, University Park, Pennsylvania. He received his B.S. and M.F. degrees from the University, and joined the faculty of the School of Forestry in 1955. He received the Ph.D. degree from Yale University in 1960. His teaching and research responsibilities are primarily in the field of forest hydrology and forest watershed management.

RICHARD H. STROUD holds the B.S. degree in biology from Bowdoin College and the M.S. degree in fisheries from the University of New Hampshire, and did graduate work at Yale and Boston Universities. He has done research in fishery management for the state of New Hampshire, the Tennessee Valley Authority, and the Massachusetts Division of Fisheries and Game. Since 1953 he has been on the staff of the Sport Fishing Institute whose executive vice-president he has been since 1955. He has written widely on fishery research and management.

JAMES B. TREFETHEN, director of publications of the Wildlife Management Institute, has been a member of the Institute staff since 1948. He is the author of two books, *Crusade for Wildlife* and *Wildlife Management and Conservation*, and has written more than one hundred articles on conservation, natural history, and outdoor recreation for national magazines. He is a graduate of Northeastern University and holds a M.S. degree in wildlife management from the University of Massachusetts.

DAVID G. WILSON, a graduate of the University of Idaho, obtained his M.S. and Ph.D. degrees from Texas A. & M. University. He was engaged in teaching and research in range management for three years at Texas A. & M. and for twelve years at the University of Arizona. In 1964 he was engaged in private range consulting associated with the Arizona Feed Consulting Service, Scottsdale, Arizona. He is now with the Bureau of Land Management, U.S. Department of the Interior, Washington, D.C. He is a charter member of the American Society of Range Management.

CONRAD L. WIRTH is a graduate of the University of Massachusetts, in landscape architecture. After five years of private practice in California and Louisiana, he served for three years with the National Capital Planning Commission. He transferred to the National Park Service in 1931, as assistant director in charge of land planning, and supervised the Department of the Interior's Civilian Conservation Corps program in the 1930's. He became director of the National Park Service in 1951 and retired in 1964. He was the author of the Park, Parkway and Recreation Study Act of 1936, and conceived MISSION 66 in 1955. He is now a consultant on conservation and park and recreation matters, and is associated with Laurance S. Rockefeller in the latter's conservation interests.

INDEX